Ottakar's LOCAL HISTOR

Banbury

Compiled by
Leila Gilholy

OTTAKAR'S

TEMPUS

First published 2001
Copyright © Ottakar's plc, 2001

Ottakar's Local History Series
produced in association with
Tempus Publishing Limited
The Mill, Brimscombe Port,
Stroud, Gloucestershire, GL5 2QG

ISBN 0 7524 2288 X

Typesetting and origination by
Tempus Publishing Limited
Printed in Great Britain by
Midway Colour Print, Wiltshire

Acknowledgements

Special thanks to Brian Little for taking time out from his busy schedule to read through and judge the entries; Martin Allitt and the staff at Banbury Local Studies Centre for their support of the project; Joseph Nunn and Martin Blinkhorn for supplying additional photographs to be included in the book; and to all those who entered the competition without whom this book would not have been possible. Thanks also to the following: Martin Smith, Stuart Lemon, Lucie Pearson, Rosie Sorrell, Julie Baines, Trudy Hedges, Helen Franklin, Charlotte Underwood, Sue Aydon, Sue Allen, Dave Green, and Andy, whose support during the project has been tremendous.

Contents

Foreword

This publication contains a number of recollections, memories, and researched pieces about the town of Banbury and its surrounding area, written by the people who live here. It resulted from a collaboration between Ottakar's Plc and Tempus Publishing; as a consequence of a local history writing competition organized by the two companies. The aim of the competition was to encourage local people to write about either some aspect of the area's history, or about their own memories or recollections of the town. The best of these were then collated and put forward for publication, with the three best entrants each winning £250.

The project, I felt, was quite an audacious one, but at the time I couldn't think of anything more exciting than being involved in the production of a local history book that had been written by local people themselves. Often, it seems, people think that their own experiences and memories are dull in comparison to others', and don't believe that they could be of interest to anyone else. The result of this is that they are often not passed on to future generations and are forgotten. In publishing the following pieces, I feel that in some way we are ensuring that a record of at least some people's experiences of history are not lost, experiences which can be read and enjoyed by future generations.

The task of reading through the entries that we received was an enjoyable one, and I would like to thank all those who contributed. Some of them made me laugh, one moved me to tears, and all were interesting to read. The entries themselves reflect many aspects of changes in Banbury and its surrounding area: some bring to life memories of a small market town with its local family traders, while others remember the war years and the expansion that occurred during the sixties, as companies began to relocate here. In addition I have included more personal memories which, while they may not be based entirely in historical fact, do portray an image of a time gone by. Lastly a book on Banbury would not be complete without village life being mentioned, nor would it be complete without accounts of notable figures that have contributed to the area in some way.

Leila Gilholy
August 2001

About the Winning Entries

Local historian Brian Little judged the competition entries, with the three winning entrants being decided as 'The Office Boy' by Alan Sargeant, 'Shoplifting' by Christine Wells and 'From Daylight to Digital: Four Generations of Photography' by Martin Blinkhorn. Included here are some comments by Brian on why he thought that these particular entries were worthy as winners.

'The Office Boy' by Alan Sargeant

This is a superb insight into the severe world of the legal support profession. It is written with feeling and has a good balance between people and the building they occupied. The article has quite a bit to say about Banbury in the late 1940s and it is possible to get a feeling for the town. Alan's entry is a worthy winner because the article is a fine cameo of the transition of school to work. It is a lively and true time-warp piece.

'Banbury Shoplifting' by Christine Wells

This pursues the themes of 'tradition and change' in a consistent and informed way. It brings alive the small family businesses which were at the heart of the town. There is also a delightful sense of sequence, tied to the way a design business moved with the times and became a catalyst for new façades in the town. Christine's article gets across the vision of Banbury as a town of small shopkeepers.

'From Daylight to Digital: Four Generations of Photography' by Martin Blinkhorn

This is a fine portrait of a family business written with passion and feeling. It is also a social 'calendar' of life at certain times, though it has to be said that some of the experiences described would have been the exception rather than the rule in Banbury. There are some superb anecdotes, especially concerning Blinkhorn's Picture Palace. Martin's article faithfully follows a family business down the generations, and complements the article by Christine.

Brian Little

During the construction of Castle Quay Shopping Centre, which opened in summer 2000.

Introduction

When asked if Banbury has changed much over the years most people would answer with a definitive yes. However, despite the truth of this reply, most changes, it seems, have really only occurred since the 1960s and 1970s when a stream of varying companies relocated here, resulting in the arrival of new families in the area. Consequently new housing estates were developed and services expanded to meet the needs of the increasing population. Prior to this Banbury remained the small market town that it had been for centuries before. It was a central point for those living in the surrounding villages to visit and obtain goods that were not sold in their village stores (often collected by the local 'carrier'), and it was characterized by its markets, its annual fair and carnival, and by the numerous long-standing family businesses that dominated trade here. Change in Banbury, probably in the same way as other small towns, has been a gradual process occurring in response to the changing demands and needs of a modern generation. Thus we now have the new Castle Quay Shopping Centre (housing numerous department stores and other shops), a variety of different restaurants and fast food outlets, and countless modern bars, all intended to meet our needs. Whilst the changes that have occurred in Banbury are an inevitable part of progress, Banbury has not lost all the characteristics reminiscent of its market town days. Whilst not as large as it once was, the market still trades on Thursdays and Saturdays; it still holds its annual fair and carnival each year; and there are still a number of long-standing family-owned businesses trading here (e.g. Blinkhorn's, Trinder's and Humphries'). The town centre, though built up over the years, still retains the basic structure that it always had; for instance it would be difficult when looking at pictures to distinguish between the North and South Bar of yesterday with those of today (minus the modern vehicles of course). If you closed your ears to the sound of the traffic as you walked down Parsons Street you could enter Ye Olde Reindeer imagining that you had been transported back in time over 300 years. Of course the Reindeer Inn is not the only old building in Banbury; S.H. Jones's shop in the High Street also dates back to the sixteenth century, and the building which housed A. Betts, the cake shop, was built in the seventeenth century. Walking through the town centre in 2001, looking at the stores with their modern shop fronts, it is easy to forget about the Banbury of the past; however, if only sometimes we took a moment to stop and look above us at some of the buildings, we would see a little of that past very much in the present.

Leila Gilholy

Ye Olde Reindeer Inn, Parsons Street, Banbury, probably during the early 1920s. This is one of the oldest buildings in Banbury, dating back to the sixteenth century.

A. Betts, the cake shop, in the early 1900s. This building is thought to date back to the seventeenth century, and it remains in 2001 a beautiful and well-maintained building.

Banbury: A Historical Sketch

Banbury has always been a progressive town; indeed a recent national newspaper quoted that 'the Cock Horse town gallops on' and it is – officially – 'the most prosperous community in Britain', with a population in 1999 of an estimated 40,000 souls (compare 12,968 in 1899 and 25,000 in the 1950s).

During the past fifty years there has been a 'change of use' of the town's facilities. Where previously it was dominated by agriculture, livestock markets, the weekly market and small family businesses, it is now an up-market financial and business centre, and is strategically placed for fast national distribution of foodstuffs via the M40 motorway, built in the 1990s. It is interesting to note that when the railway opened in Banbury in 1893 (which ended the post coach service run by J. Drinkwater daily from the George and Dragon), the train fare was 17s 6d, and the journey only took two and a half hours. Although the delights of open countryside still beckon the town dweller, and are literally minutes away, Banbury itself now has much to offer the visitor, yet is also centrally placed for visits to other favourite scenic/shopping haunts a short ride away in the delightful Warwickshire and Northamptonshire countryside.

Banbury was founded 1,500 years ago by the Saxons, and then played host to the Danes who established the market. However it was the Normans who built extensively in Banbury. The town suffered great damage in the seventeenth century, first in a fire in 1628 and then during the Civil War in the 1640s, when many houses were intentionally demolished or destroyed by fire and gunfire. In fact, only two buildings still remain which predate the seventeenth century: the Reindeer Inn and the house on the west side of the Market Place on the corner of Butchers Row.

No one thinks of Banbury without thinking of Banbury Cross and the famous nursery rhyme. The original town cross was destroyed in the early seventeenth century (it is thought by Puritans) and the current cross was erected in 1859. Banbury was also home to a central castle (where Oliver Cromwell is said to have encountered a Royalist party defending it in 1655), and was the location for the renowned Battle of Cropredy Bridge.

Banbury was always busy: in the thirteenth century a community of drapers, wool-weavers and cheese-makers began the earliest cottage industries. Brewing has been carried on in the town since the Middle Ages (the most successful brewer being Thomas Hunt, since 1847). There is also Brown's famous sixteenth-century 'Banbury Cake' and countless carriers' carts transported produce from rural areas to and from the Thursday and Saturday markets. These markets are still vibrant and dictate the rhythm of the town. It stirs the soul to walk the streets where sheep, cattle and horse markets were held in the open streets of the town: cattle on alternate Thursdays in the Cow Fair (Bridge Street), horses on the west side of Horsefair, and sheep penned at the top of the High Street. Dealers mainly conducted their business in the Crown Hotel in Bridge Street or the Market Place Exchange, and in 1925 the Midland Marts took over the auctioning of animals. The first dealers' market emerged on the Midland Marts' Grimsbury site in 1931. The livestock fairs in Banbury culminated in the largest livestock market in Europe during the 1930s, but an era of Banbury's history sadly ended with its closure in June 1998.

Becoming an 'adopted Banburian' after fifty-five years of living here, it is nice to be associated with some of the good things life has on offer at the turn of the century. Quoted in the *Banbury Guardian* on 30 July 2000, a returning visitor commented, 'Banbury turned out to be a town way beyond childhood memories – was it really a trip or was it a dream?'

Edna Sparkes

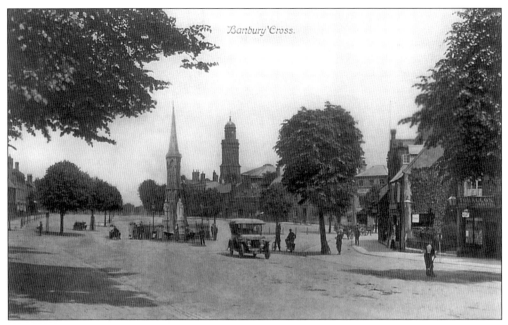

Banbury Cross, seen from South Bar, probably c. 1920. The statues that surround the monument were not added for at least fifty years after the cross was erected. In the distance, along North Bar, the tower of St Mary's church can be seen.

The Town Hall from Bridge Street, at the turn of the twentieth century.

CHAPTER 1
Local Businesses

Thomas and Norman Blinkhorn with their Darracq car in 1912. This was the second car in Banbury.

Top left: *The studios of portrait photographers often contained elaborate settings such as this one. Here, Edith Blinkhorn and a friend pose in their Victorian dresses, c. 1880.*

Top right: *Norman Blinkhorn, aged about four years, photographed by his father using only daylight. Thomas Blinkhorn traded under the name of A. Beales Ltd from 1883 to 1916 at the Parade Studio in South Bar.*

Norman Blinkhorn posing with his mother Edith.

From Daylight to Digital: Four Generations of Photography

My grandfather, Thomas Jeffer Blinkhorn, never quite came to terms with electricity. When he set up as a photographer in 1880 he used daylight to expose his glass plates and made his photographs in the same way, arranging his printing-frames in the yard outside his studio in South Bar, praying that the sun would shine. In the safety of his darkroom he would develop his negatives and prints in porcelain dishes, measuring out the developer and hypo from large demijohns in which he had mixed the powdered chemicals. His studio, a large wooden building with elaborate backgrounds and heavy furniture, had an enormous glass skylight to illuminate his sitters who were required to pose for seconds at a time, usually dressed in their Sunday best. Artificial light was provided by gaslight and later by arc lights, but until the day he died (in 1947) he never 'switched off the electricity' – he always referred to it as 'turning off the gas'. Before going out to take photographs around the villages he would harness his pony and trap, load up with a darkroom tent, bottles of chemicals, and heavy mahogany and brass cameras and tripods. On arriving he would pitch his tent and set about the task of mixing light-sensitive emulsions to coat the glass plates. When dry plates were invented and he no longer needed a lightproof tent he bought a Darracq car (registration number BW1066), only the second in Banbury, and drove it himself until his son, Norman, obtained a licence in 1912. This was a relief to everyone because Thomas preferred to drive

The Blinkhorn family in 1907. From left to right: Thomas, Bernard, Edith (née Aspell) and Norman.

Blinkhorn's Picture House in Market Place, which was run by Thomas and his family.

House. A number of the films were serials like *The Perils of Pauline* with a different episode every week usually involving Pauline being tied to a railway track or being carried off by a licentious sheikh into the desert. The most popular film was *The Kid* starring Charlie Chaplin and it ran for several weeks. Thomas judged how frightening a film was by feeling the benches in the front row; if they were damp he knew the story had been terrifying. Sound effects were produced backstage behind the silver screen and Bernard, Thomas's youngest son, once lost control of a huge steel drum used to simulate landslides and it rolled through the screen into the orchestra pit trapping

on the right-hand side of the road; as he put it, 'I can see more easily what's coming towards me'. Light was most essential to him and his profession depended on it. He was a skilled photographer and many thousands of his sepia photographs survive to this day.

In 1907 he opened Blinkhorn's Picture House, the first cinema in Banbury, situated in the Market Place, and for three days each week showed silent films with Nellie Alcock providing the piano accompaniment assisted by the occasional musician. On the other three days the stage was used for travelling fit-up shows and during the First World War audiences usually contained a proportion of wounded soldiers recuperating after being injured in the trenches of France.

Thomas's daughter-in-law, Dorothy, ran the box office while her husband, Norman, was away in the Army (he was Winston Churchill's dispatch-rider until he fell off his motorbike and joined the Flying Corps), and she told many stories of the Picture

Norman Blinkhorn joined the Army in 1914 and for a short while was a motorcycle dispatch-rider for Winston Churchill. He later joined the Royal Flying Corps.

Nellie against her piano, and causing a hasty evacuation of the front row.

Dorothy's dog was a scruffy terrier called Tim who would sleep each evening in front of the gas fire in the box office and when Nellie played the National Anthem at the end of the performance he would get up, stretch, and then scavenge for the scraps of fish and chips left amongst the cinema seats. When the Armistice was declared in 1918, Thomas announced the news from the stage before the evening's performance and in a burst of patriotic fervour Nellie and her small band struck up the National Anthem and the entire audience sang 'God Save the King'. Tim had just settled down in front of the gas fire on this cold November evening and hearing the drum roll and the National Anthem played – leapt to his feet and ran

barking round the auditorium, confused and unable to find any fish and chips. Like Pavlov's dog, he was never the same again!

Norman was invalided out of the Royal Flying Corps and came back into the family business, gradually taking over from his father whose eyesight was deteriorating, forcing him to do less photography and concentrate on frame-making, working almost entirely from feel and memory. His passion for straightening small nails led to him having very bent fingers and a shortened temper. The 1920s came and went for the younger Blinkhorns in a frenzy of tennis parties, amateur theatricals, the Charleston and motoring down to the beach-hut at Bournemouth. *The Jazz Singer* brought sound to Hollywood movies and, unable to afford the expense of conversion,

Thomas and Edith Blinkhorn in their lounge above the shop premises where they lived from 1883 to 1942.

the old Picture House was reluctantly sold to a consortium and became the Palace Cinema with motor-driven projectors, loudspeakers, plush tip-up seats and ice-cream girls. The gas fire was taken out of the box office and Tim was now getting too old to go to the pictures. He drowned swimming across the canal – probably looking for fish and chips! In 1930, the year I was born, a disastrous fire destroyed the wooden studio building in South Bar; a large amount of equipment was damaged and most of the collection of glass negatives lost. Thomas

Norman Blinkhorn was involved in many community affairs including the Borough Council, Banbury Rotary Club and the Scout Association. In 1938 he was National President of the Institute of Photographers, lecturing all round the UK and broadcasting on the BBC.

stood amongst the debris and wept. The fire, which had destroyed his beloved studio, also destroyed the fire in his heart and I don't think he ever took another photograph. The country was going through a depression and builders were looking for work as they had been laid off from the Easington development where a housing estate was being built for workers at the newly formed Northern Aluminium Company factory. William Morris (later Lord Nuffield) had worked with Thomas and he loaned him the money to build a new studio and darkroom-block using builders who had been laid off. By this time Thomas's eyesight was very poor. Eventually he lost his sight almost completely and retired from active photographic work.

Another studio was opened in Evesham, run by his youngest son, Bernard Laxton Blinkhorn, and Norman with his wife Dorothy at his side took over the rebuilt studio, together with the shop in South Bar. He expanded into 16mm film-making and retailing cameras and equipment. Norman had always been interested in cinema and ran a mobile unit showing films in some of the big houses in the area and helping keen amateurs make 16mm films. At that time John Profumo lived at Avon Dassett and he made several films with the aid of Norman who also helped him build a small cinema in the stables at Avon Carrow. This was visited by many stars of the cinema including Marlene Dietrich, Douglas Fairbanks and Valerie Hobson (who later married John Profumo). All these visitors signed a drainpipe in the building, later destroyed during conversion.

Norman was a frequent visitor to Upton House where he showed films for Lord Bearsted and visited other local stately homes, particularly for the Christmas

Staff at Blinkhorn's in 1952. From left to right, back row: Tony Hazewood, Pamela Stockley, Pauline Parkinson, Betty Hart, Gordon Barker. Front row: Martin Blinkhorn, Dorothy Blinkhorn, Molly Ruffhead (with Virginia Barker), Norman Blinkhorn, Mary Barker.

festivities. At one of these visits he was asked to wait while the guests finished dinner, the butler serving him with a large glass of brandy and an equally large cigar. To while away the time Norman tried to converse with the parrot which lived in a large ornate cage in the hall, but the parrot was uncommunicative and to show its displeasure snatched the smoking cigar from his hand and promptly ate it. The parrot fell on its back with both feet in the air and died instantly while Norman stood back astounded. The butler was not surprised, commenting, 'Well, that's probably the first parrot to die of smoking'.

Thomas, who had survived his wife Edith, spent his last few years trying to understand the radio, smoking one ounce of tobacco and going through ten boxes of Swan matches every week; and enjoying sugar lumps soaked in strictly medicinal whisky. By this time he was virtually blind and took an hour to dress in the mornings. He would snooze in his favourite armchair between filling and trying to light his pipe, and would go for short walks along the footpath in Bloxham Road, speaking to everyone and recognizing no one. When asked if he would like a white walking stick he replied, 'No thank you, I don't think I could see it.' He liked to smuggle an electric fire under the dining table to warm his slippers and occasionally set fire to himself. Like all old photographers he didn't die, he just went out of focus. When he was nearly ninety he fell down stairs and almost unhurt went reluctantly into the Horton Hospital. Mont Hirons of Bloxham was in the next bed to him and Thomas offered him his evening meal which Mont, a young and hungry man, eagerly accepted. When he took the plate back, Thomas had slipped away, quietly and with no fuss, rather in the way he had lived his life. Thomas was very proud of his father, a platinotype photographer whose own father before him had invented a roundabout where the horses went up and down as well as round and round. Thomas had a fairground poster advertising 'Blinkhorn's Galloping Horses', and in his

drawing room he also had a Victorian plaque which read 'Don't worry, it may never happen' and for Thomas Jeffer Harmond Blinkhorn I don't think it ever did. He left behind a changed world and countless sepia photographs of people and places, reminding us of the way things were, once upon a time.

The Second World War saw the photographic business doing its bit for the war effort. Young men who had worked in the darkrooms went off to the RAF, the Army and the Royal Navy, some of them never to return. Norman, himself helping to run the Air Training Corps, photographed many hundreds of men and women in uniform, providing likenesses which stood on the mantelpiece to remind loved ones of sons who were fighting in countries they knew nothing of, or who were in prisoner of

Aircraftman Martin Blinkhorn shows off in front of a Vampire during his National School of Photography days.

Martin Blinkhorn served in the Royal Air Force School of Photography.

war camps in Germany. There were secret things to be photographed for the War Office – camouflaged factories, bomb damage, experimental jet aircraft at Barford St John and outboard motors for D-Day landing craft being tested in a church building in the centre of Banbury. Our family home in Bloxham Road was always full of RAF aircrew; many were from the Commonwealth and almost every night there was a party with Americans, Canadians and Australians usually bringing food parcels from their homes overseas. We drank beer and played riotous games, dancing to records of Glenn Miller and Louis Armstrong and smooching with the girls who preferred Bing Crosby and Dinah Shore. Mary, my nineteen-year-old sister, had married an RAF fighter pilot who flew his Hurricane over the house and waggled his wings to indicate there was going to be another party tonight if he could fiddle the petrol to drive from RAF Silverstone. Food was rationed, petrol almost non-existent, sweets, beer and cigarettes in short supply, but in some ways life was vibrant and full of hope. In 1945 at Christmas my mother planned a big reunion for the young men of the family who were returning from the war. Three of her nephews were never to return and I think it was the last of the big wartime parties as by this time the old country had spent all its money and there followed ten years of austerity.

Blinkhorn's is and was a truly family business. With Norman at the helm and Dorothy as his first mate, my brother-in-law Gordon Barker joined us, recovering from injuries sustained when his fighter plane was shot down, and my sister Mary became an excellent colourist. We were always blessed with a magnificent staff without which no business can survive. As soon as I left school I started at the 'grass roots', training for a year in the darkrooms with Fred Fosbury and John Fletcher, both of whom had been in the RAF and who persuaded me to do the same. So at seventeen I joined the Air Force and was fortunate to be accepted by the RAF School of Photography where I enjoyed myself enormously, receiving superb training, scrounging petrol to run my old Aston Martin sports car and being flown all over the place mainly to play squash for Technical Training Command at far-away air bases. The station commander was a pre-war racing driver and 'volunteered' me to take him to motor races on old airfields. I spent a lot of time photographing VIPs at important events and made friends with some of the top press photographers from London newspapers. This stood me in good stead when I was demobbed in 1950 and came back to Banbury and the family photographic business where I have spent fifty happy years doing what my grandfather and father did before me.

My son, another Thomas Jeffer Blinkhorn, has now taken over the running of the business, developing it along the hi-tech electronic road that is opening up before us. What would his great grandfather have thought (as he took his sepia portraits in a studio without electricity) if he had been told that one day his great-grandson could take a colour photograph on a digital camera the size of a cigarette packet and send it to Australia in a few seconds? He might have said, 'Don't worry – it may never happen!' But it did.

Martin Blinkhorn
Prize-winning entry

Percy Gilkes promoting his business at one of the many trade shows that took place around the area.

Annie Catherine (née Newton), wife of Percy Gilkes. Percy was an enthusiastic photographer in those days and developed his own films.

Granny Newton and Percy Gilkes in the garden at the back of the General Store in Warwick Road. This has since been demolished and is now the side of the current police station.

The Newsagency and General Store

I was born in 1926, the year of the General Strike, at No. 32 Parsons Street, which is now Dillon's. The photograph (p. 25) shows my father outside the shop in the 1930s. He, Percy Gilkes, started the news agency after training as a compositor. At the beginning he carried on with his trade as a printer whilst Mother kept the shop ticking over. During the ensuing years it went from strength to strength and finished up supplying wholesale and retail outlets over a wide area. My father was a staunch union man and a founder member of the Banbury Labour Party. He served on the Town Council until ill health forced him to resign; his political activities were recorded in the

book *Over the Hills to Glory*. In the 1945 election I ferried the Labour Party agent around the North Oxfordshire constituency to village meetings, which were usually held outside on village greens and more often than not were very lively affairs.

I loved helping in the shop when I was not at school and eventually worked there full-time until I married and started a family. (Incidentally after we moved to Twyford, we ran our own newspaper business.)

My father had a small printing press at the top of the shop where he did small jobs, e.g. business cards, programmes, stationery etc. On Saturday nights during the football season, it was a hive of activity. One must remember that at this time television was in its infancy and wirelesses were a luxury. It was my father's job to print the football results into the 'Stop Press' section of the evening papers. Earlier in the day he would have assembled the teams in position so that when the results started coming through from London he was able to fill in the results. These were then printed into the 'Stop Press' and I loved to race down the stairs with the results to the eagerly awaiting customers who would have gathered around the shop. How things have changed! My father would not recognize the enormous advances which have been made with the printed word. Most children today have access to a computer and it is amazing how quickly they become competent. I think they probably enjoy their IT lessons more than anything else. All businesses are benefiting from their expertise as stocktaking, accounts, and records can all be easily stored making the life of business people so much easier.

We were a large family – five boys and five girls. Think of all the washing, ironing, cooking and washing up! During the war years my mother must have had a very difficult time, with the food shortages, but I can never remember being hungry.

My Granny Newton had a little general store along the Warwick Road where the new police station now stands. She sold all kinds of things and a wide variety of sweets. In my mind I can only ever remember her wearing black. Years ago people always wore black as a sign of respect if someone died. We were frequent visitors to the shop on our way to and from St Mary's School in

Percy Gilkes outside his news agency at the top of Parsons Street in the 1930s. The store still trades as a newsagent today.

Harold Gilkes, Grampy Gilkes and Grace Gilkes at No. 156 Broughton Road. Grace remembers the watch well: it didn't work!

shops opening and everything carrying on as normal.

During the war we had evacuees for a time. The family that we had staying with us had been in some very bad air raids in London, and were very nervous when the sirens went off. They eventually returned to London. They couldn't seem to settle in what to them must have seemed a very quiet backwater.

Banbury has become quite cosmopolitan in recent years with workers moving here from London, Birmingham and immigrants from overseas. It will be interesting to see what effect the M40 will have on the town in the future. I feel very privileged to have lived in and around Banbury all by life. It is a unique town with a character all of its own.

Grace Plester

Banbury 'Shoplifting'

A Tribute to the shopfitting firm of Randolph Harper, who designed and transformed many of Banbury's retail premises between 1935 and 1992.

We lost count of the number of people who humorously, or genuinely, misread our designation on the firm's vehicles. 'Shopfitting' it said; 'Shoplifting' they read. In a way both were true: we did give a face-lift to Banbury's shops for over fifty years. Randolph Harper trained and then taught at Banbury Art School in Marlborough Road (then known as Banbury Technical Institute and School of Art) and began his freelance career as a commercial artist. Those advertisements above the parcel rack in

Southam Road. The shop had a stable-type door and a bell used to clang loudly as one entered. Granny would come bustling in from the kitchen where she always seemed to be working. We were allowed to have a halfpennyworth of broken sweets and it was put on the slate which Mother would settle every Friday. Monday was the day to call if you wanted some of her famous Yorkshire pudding; I've never been able to bake one like it!

We were expected to go to Sunday school and my Granny Newton frowned on us if we did any knitting or sewing, as Sunday was a day of rest. Playing out in the street was also frowned upon. It is sad that Sunday has become the same as any other day with

Blinkhorn's new shop front, which was designed by Randolph Harper during the late 1930s.

Charles's bus from Middleton Cheney, and the show cards and sale tickets for Judges, the drapers in the High Street, were some of his first jobs. I followed in his footsteps and wrote sale tickets too, as an art student from õ. 51 The Green in the 1960s.

The High Street of the 1940s and '50s was quite different at shop front level to that of today. Most of the shops were locally owned and often the proprietor lived above the premises. Whether 'modernization' was a good thing or not will always be a matter for conjecture; the trend now is to re-create the shop fronts of the nineteenth century, but in the reconstruction time following the Second World War, our clients were looking for a new face: plate glass, so the customer could actually see inside, improved lighting and the new wonder of self-service and

A sale ticket from Judges the drapers, where Randolph Harper had one of his first jobs.

South Bar, looking down to Banbury Cross, in the early twentieth century. In the right-hand corner of the picture we can see two ladies looking through the window of Beales' photographic shop. (Supplied by Martin Blinkhorn)

Before and after the renovation of the shop front of Fredrick Anker Ltd in the 1980s.

This photograph, looking down the High Street, was taken at the time of Queen Elizabeth's Jubilee in 1977. Mrs Usher owned all these businesses and the frontages were designed by Randolph Harper.

accessibility to the goods were all the vogue. Local stone with hardwood window frames for the smaller shop, mosaics, laminates and aluminium for the larger units – these were the customer's general requirements. Often we disagreed but the customer is always right and the Town and Country Planning Department had the last word anyway.

Many of the family firms are now long gone, but one of the earliest to which my father gave his attention is the still thriving photographic business of Blinkhorn's in South Bar. This business was formerly Beales, but it was Mr Norman Blinkhorn who commissioned Randolph Harper's Art Deco design for the shop front, which was largely pre-fabricated and applied over the existing structure. A further re-fit in more recent years has now obscured this work, but

that's progress and in the field of design nothing stands still.

These were the days when a chair was provided beside the counter, often a high one as I recall; thus the older customer could rest while an assistant fulfilled her order. As a child I watched in fascination as Judges' high-wire tramway transported money to the cashier's office at the back of the shop and moments later whirred back again across the ceiling carrying the required change and receipt.

Access to many of the shops was poor, up several steps, or as in the Market Place post office, the floor was uneven, with boards with raised knots and nail heads polished by the customers' tread. The knot-holes were of enormous interest to a bored child in a queue.

Randolph Harper with the gold tap that he designed for Hunt Edmund Brewery, 1960.

Over the years many of the street frontages have been re-styled. Often this was a necessity and considerable work to strengthen the façades took place before our cosmetic work could begin. Almost every shop in Parsons Street had a well under its retail area. This were discovered so often it was no longer a panic when a hole appeared. Work stopped briefly when foundations for the re-styled front of Fields Department Store, Church Lane, were dug. Overnight some joker had placed animal bone, acquired most likely from Fowler's the butchers nearby, in the hole.

Probably the biggest reconstruction undertaken was to the entire façade of Anker's Insurance building at 32 High Street. Before the shop front could be replaced all the exterior walls had to be tied

Messrs Watts & Sons at the Oxfordshire Show in the 1950s. The agricultural show stand was another of Randolph Harper's designs.

Market Place in 1973, just before the building of the Castle Shopping Centre.

Market Place, looking down towards the Palace Arcade (previously Blinkhorn's Picture House) in 1973.

in to the rest of the building. The distinctive clock remained in position throughout but I don't think we can claim to have kept it running.

One of Randolph Harper's most loyal customers was Mrs Ethel Usher, from Watson's wine merchants at No. 39 High Street before 1950, the Inn Within in 1951, the Winston Restaurant, the Windsor Coffee Shop, and Watson's Fine Food Market, the last at No. 2 Horsefair. Most memorable, though, to a generation looking for entertainment, was the Winter Gardens, which stood between 1956 and 1982 behind the shops that made up Mrs Usher's empire. We were involved in the design and fitting of all of these, right down to the emergency

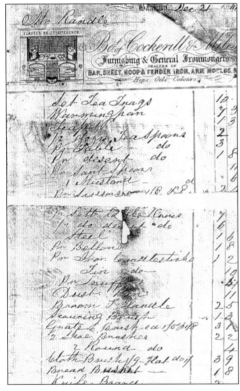

An invoice from Messrs Cockerill & Miles, dated 21 December 1869.

maintenance such as replacing the wire rope of the dumb waiter when it had launched a dozen dinners to their doom on a busy Bank Holiday Monday in the Winston Restaurant.

This was a time for experimenting with new materials. Plastic replaced aluminium and wood for most shop front letters; stainless steel and bronzed aluminium extrusions for frames; and for exhibitions and displays all these could be used almost without restriction, the only limitation being the imagination of the designer. Around 1959 Hunt Edmunds, the local brewery, launched a new brew called Gold Tap. We were called upon to produce a six-foot long model tap to display on top of a vehicle. This we duly fabricated from obeche wood and gilded. For the accompanying signwork another tap of similar dimensions was cut out by hot wire from that wonderful new material, polystyrene, which at the time every handyman was blithely sticking on the ceiling, unaware of the fire hazard. I well remember pouring Evo Stick on the back to glue it to a signboard and seeing the adhesive eat the polystyrene right through to the gold leaf face.

Exhibition work largely revolved around the summertime agricultural shows. The Oxfordshire Show and The Royal Show were nomadic in the 1940s and early '50s and sometimes visited Banbury, when the venue was a field close by the present-day Bodicote flyover. Our local customers were Watts & Sons and Twyford Mill (later Bibby's) at Adderbury. Mrs Watts was particularly proud of her hospitality marquee (supplied by Plumbs, Market Place). This would be lined with swathes of muslin in pastel shades and would have large, artistic floral displays within.

A team of Randolph Harper's employees, from left to right: Robin Clifton, Joe Barter, John Adey, Chris Cliffton, Irene Harvey and Vernon Luckett.

Exhibitions were transient work; prefabricated for speed on site and designed to look good and appeal to the public for a few days each year. The shops, of course, were intended for longer life. Many in the 1960s and '70s came and went but several names with which we were associated lived on through several decades and called us back from time to time to bring them up to date. In Parsons Street, M. Bernard Smith, drapers and haberdashers, Knott the pie-man and W.A. Truss the fishmongers stood the test of time; as did Railton's shoe shop in the High Street, Ankers, Goggin & Baker, stationers, and Mrs Usher's empire. To date, the only unchanged frontages that remain are Ankers, ex-Railtons, the windows (but not the signwork) of A Plan, and Church's China.

The Market Place saw a huge revolution in shopping when the Castle Centre was developed behind the existing Market Place façades on the north side. Few smaller local retailers went into this new shopping mall and multi-national companies or groups' own fitters carried out the majority of fitting.

Across on the west side of the Market Place a minor revolution was tried by Mr Mansfield when he acquired the Palace Arcade. This was the entrance to the Palace Cinema (now HSBC bank) and is probably well remembered by an older generation as the premises of Mr Hubert Peake, dentist, in whose chair they would have spent an uncomfortable half-hour. When we were called in to transform the cinema interior into a mega toyshop in preparation for Christmas trade, there was still an aura of grandeur about the Palace. The raked floors were a headache to build level counters on; the ante-rooms and dressing rooms below the cinema screen stage still contained items from theatrical use; but best of all was the opportunity to go out onto the roof for a pigeon's-eye view of the Market Place prior to its redevelopment, when the Apple Tree Tea Rooms, the Prime Meat Company and Durran's the jewellers still occupied the shops on the north side.

Bringing tired and run down properties back to life with a new face has been a rewarding job and since the business closed in 1992 I have had the opportunity to do a lot of reminiscence work with the elderly. Whatever subjects we start out on we almost always find ourselves walking down memory lanes in Banbury. Now it is difficult for me to recognize which are my own memories and which have been relayed to me. Pilsworth's and McIlroy's in Parsons Street are before my time but Kingerlee's and Dossett's I remember well.

It is interesting to note how just a few properties have supported the same kind of trade over the years. E. Railton was a boot and shoemaker at No. 13 High Street as far back as 1837. In the Market Place we worked on Robins Bros Ltd, ironmongers, at No. 16. This is now an outlet for the Cargo chain and you can still by saucepans and kettles as you could in 1869 when the premises were occupied by Messrs Cockerill and Miles, furnishing and general ironmongers. One might have to visit an antique shop now for the warming pan and iron fender (priced at 7s 3d and 2s 3d respectively) and the hatchet at 1s 9d as listed on an invoice of theirs for December 1869.

As a 'hospital job' for when business was slow or a job was held up outside our control, Randolph Harper designed his own house at Balscote. The concept was based on minimum external walling for maximum internal space, and he would demonstrate this with a cigarette packet. A packet of twenty if squeezed into a cylinder, would hold more than twice as many cigarettes; so the house is octagonal. Three double bedrooms, bathroom, lounge, hall and kitchen/diner, having large windows glazed with shop-plate to give an open feel to the rooms. Had the money and technology been available in the 1950s, my father would really have liked to put the whole house on a turntable for maximum light and sunshine. The skills of stonemason builders Chris Clifton and his son Robin, in turn foremen of the shopfitting gang, were tested and not found wanting in the building of the octagonal house. Mr Clifton Snr's grandfather had reconstructed an arch in Shenington church and Mr Clifton Jnr's son now continues the skill of stonemason in the area.

Local shops were fitted by local businesses and tradesmen and suppliers were mainly local too. There was Hood, the ironmongers; Cleaver's in George Street for pipes and glass; Plumb's in Market Place supplied rope and canvas; Friswell's for steel; and the blacksmith would make up an odd-sized brace or tie or bolt; and for all those intricate little odds and ends not found in anyone's catalogue or on their shelves, there was always Herbert Tooley at the boat yard on the canal, whose ingenuity often saved the day. It is fitting that Banbury's new museum is being built to encompass this area of industry past.

Christine Wells
Prize-winning entry

CHAPTER 2
A Market Town

Adderbury Co-op in the 1930s. It continued to trade up until its closure in 1978.

The High Street in the 1920s. On the right is the Red Lion pub, with the red lion statue above the frontage

Banbury Market Place, late 1940s. This photograph was taken from the roof of the Palace Cinema, and while none of the businesses here remain, the buildings mostly do. At the far end of Market Place is the Bear Inn. This was later regarded by some as being quite a rough pub, but today it is the site of a prominent High Street chain. (Supplied by Martin Blinkhorn)

Memories of Banbury

Going to Banbury in the late 1920s and early '30s was considered to be a special treat, even though I grew up in Adderbury, which was only 3 miles away. We had almost all that we needed in the village with a Co-op, two high-class grocers, and another small shop that sold everything including groceries, sweets, tobacco, second-hand pots and pans and even the odd piece of furniture. There was also a butcher's shop and two bakeries who, before electricity came, would cook the Sunday dinner in their bread ovens. About three times a week the bakers would deliver their lovely home-made loaves, the milkman would call with large buckets of milk which he would measure into a jug with a pint or half-pint measure, and Amos the butcher brought meat round in his van twice a week. There was also Billy Hobs, known as the oilman, but he brought much more than the paraffin needed for light and cooking. His van was a travelling hardware store with polishes of every description, brushes, brooms, mats, candles, spare parts for oil stoves, tin kettles, saucepans, or maybe a pot mender to mend an old one. As he bowled along the streets his goods would rattle and bang together and sometimes fall off the back. Another reason for not going into town was that the 'carrier' Will Howes would bring back anything that was needed for twopence, less than half the bus fare, which I believe was fourpence halfpenny return.

One of my first memories of Banbury was of my dad lifting me up in the High Street and asking me if I could see the big Red Lion. When I said that I could, he said 'you remember that you saw it as they are going to knock it down to build a Woolworth's. That would have been about 1930. The building of Woolworth's caused great excitement as it introduced a new way of shopping. People had not been used to picking up their own purchases; in other shops goods were kept behind the counter and had to be asked for and placed on the counter by the assistants. I was taken to Woolworth's shortly after it opened and all I could see was the high dark brown-varnished counters; I was much too small to see the goods. Everything was either threepence or sixpence. Sandals or plimsolls would be sixpence for each shoe. At that time they sold almost anything. In fact there was a couple of quite elderly village characters that had been courting for a good many years, and when at last Eva persuaded her Sam to tie the knot he complained bitterly that he had to pay seven and a tanner (7s 6d) for a wedding ring not long before Woolworth's opened. It was said that if he hadn't have been in such a hurry he could have bought one in Woolworth's for sixpence. On Saturdays there was such a crowd in there that it was a job to fight your way around.

Of course I did appreciate Woolworth's when I got older, especially as we could buy so many things at a reasonable price, as we could see exactly how much everything cost before parting with our pocket money or later hard-earned wages. At one time they had a milk bar and we would treat ourselves to a chocolate milkshake on payday.

Banbury Fair was considered a great event for both young and old; it was the only time some of the older generation came into Banbury. It was quite a gathering of the clans as people pushed their way through the crowds looking for relatives and friends that they had probably not seen since the year before. The biggest crush was usually outside the boxing booth. I can remember

Maud Hawkins, Ivy Hawkins, Alfred Hawkins, Levi Hawkins (front), David Taylor and Rhoda Hawkins, in the early 1930s.

being lifted up to see the Turpin brothers wearing their gloves and shorts and challenging anyone to try to beat them. I believe there was a considerable cash reward but I don't think many chaps managed to win it. It was a novelty to hear the music, and to see the bright coloured lights and the big steam engines that powered them. When we had had our rides Mam would say she hadn't any money left and that we would have to catch the bus home; however, she would sometimes discover that she had enough money left to call at Needles for fish and chips to take home. Once I remember that we actually ate them at a table in the shop. The first time I went to the pictures was what should have been a trip to the fair. It started to bucket down with rain so my mam took me into the Palace Cinema. The film was *The End of the Road*, starring Harry Lauder, I believe.

My Dad did not approve of going to the pictures. He said that everybody who had been off work bad went to the pictures and you could catch anything. The only thing I remember catching was the odd flea, which was quite a common occurrence and the bites were a nasty itch until the flea was caught. However, he could be persuaded to take me to see George Formby.

As I got older I was allowed to go to Banbury to the Saturday afternoon matinée if there was a suitable film on. I remember going to see *Victoria the Great*. There used to be a man standing outside the Grand in Broad Street with a brown uniform trimmed with gold buttons and braid. He used to shout, 'Fourpence and sixpence in the queue, tuppence round Pepper Alley!'. There was always a lot of noise and some of the kids used to try and sneak in through the back way, and sometimes we would see them

Oxford Road from the High Street in Adderbury. The post office and the Wheatsheaf pub have since closed. Rhoda Hawkins and her family lived in the cottage on the far left of the photograph.

Adderbury Methodist church Sunday school outing, 1937. From left to right, back row: David Chowiv, Mr George Humphris (Sunday school superintendent), Mrs Adkins, Mrs Davis, Connie Adkins, Violet Stanton, Kit Wolton, Mrs Smith. Front row: Eric Smith, Rhoda Hawkins, Sue Hawkins, Margaret Padbury and Betty Davis.

Part of the right-hand side of Market Place, looking down towards the Town Hall building. It shows the Fox Inn, Hills & Rowney (the first art shop in Banbury), and Neal's shoe store. Above them is the site of the old Gaol. (Supplied by Martin Blinkhorn)

being taken out. I did not often go myself but I believe the Saturday morning kids' shows were even noisier.

Although the villagers did not depend on the town for food they would have needed to buy clothing and shoes. The Co-op was, I would think, the nearest we had to a department store, and sold almost everything in the drapery line. Children were not often taken to choose their clothes; mothers would buy what they thought was suitable. A lot of our clothes were homemade and Pilsworth' had a good selection of materials. Our school had a clothing club, which meant children paid a few coppers each week and when the

schools broke up in July the vouchers would be issued. Mam always had ours made out to the Co-op as they sold shoes as well as the other drapery.

Living in a village there were quite a few things we found different in the town. I remember being taken to the town's toilets; the flush toilets and stiff white squares of toilet paper in white china holders were a novelty to some of the country folk. Not forgetting the enamel notices offering a substantial reward for 'information on anyone using these toilets suffering from venereal disease'. I did not understand anything except the reward and once asked my Mam how we could obtain what seemed to me to be a small fortune and was quickly dragged outside. There was always an attendant with her mops, Brasso and cleaning cloths, and all the taps were highly polished. I am sure she would have been capable of dealing with anyone who threatened to damage her domain.

Unless a child had been fortunate to pass the scholarship and go to what was then known as Banbury County School the rest of us left school at the age of fourteen. My turn came in July 1939. My mother had a small teashop so I did not go to work straight away. It was a lovely summer. I had a stall outside and I sold what must have been hundreds of soft drinks and ice creams. A great may people went on cycling holidays and I remember a sense of foreboding as they were saying that they were making the most of this year as there would be a war. Soon we were measured and issued with gas masks and sandbags, and paper strips appeared on all the windows in the town. A few weeks later we were at war and our village had a whole battalion of soldiers arrive, with huts springing up in what almost seemed overnight.

After a couple of years Mam closed the shop and I went to work at Spencer's corset factory, where there were very strict rules, with no talking allowed on the benches. We made surgical corsets and belts. This was when I really began to love Banbury. I met girls my own age and began to go to the Saturday night dances at the Town Hall where we danced to well known bands of that time. There were crowds of RAF personnel coming into the town from several surrounding airfields, as well as all the soldiers, so there was no shortage of partners and surprisingly not very much trouble. There was no alcohol sold on the premises, but we were all quite happy with

Wincott's Café, South Bar, 1938. During the Second World War American soldiers were billeted here. (Supplied by Martin Blinkhorn)

the powdered lemonade or coffee and a sausage roll. In spite of clothes rationing we always managed to look nice. We queued at the market stalls in our dinner hour or on Saturdays for makeup or curtain material to make into a blouse. Many a lad came home on leave to find his grey flannel trousers had been made into a skirt by one of his sisters. One time a stall came with a lot of bomb damaged Celanese underwear, mostly camiknickers all soaking wet and sooty but only needing half coupons. They certainly would have been too expensive for us to buy in new condition. However, they washed up nice and clean and we really appreciated them. It was also possible to buy seconds in silk stockings (nylons had not come our way then) and after careful examination; it was possible to find some where the mend did not show. Thus we had many devious ways of stretching our clothing coupons.

As well as the dances in other villages and Town Halls there were the three picture houses, The Grand in Broad Street with double seats at the back for courting couples, the Palace in the Market Place (now a bank), and the Regal, which is now the only one left out of the three, and now has another name.

With so many of the armed forces coming into the town there were always long queues to get in, but that was all part of the fun. There were several good musicals and we watched Betty Grable, Alice Faye and all the glamorous film stars; we fell in love with the men and dreamed we could look like the girls. When the Pathé News came on we booed the Italian and German soldiers and cheered our boys.

It was a sad time and a romantic time, and it was easy to fall in love with the boys in uniform, with a strange feeling knowing that maybe in a few weeks or less they could be killed in action. We also heard the same of lads we had known all our lives.

Even during the war years there was a fairly good bus from Adderbury, both into Banbury or Oxford, the last bus being at 10.30 p.m. Most of the time I used to cycle, as bikes could be left at Caves store in Bridge Street and collected quite late on dance nights. I think he charged us about 6d. Front lamps had to be half covered with black paper and the street lamps where there were any were very dim, but we still managed to find our way around quite safely.

When I was seventeen and a half I had to register for war service and because of Mam's tearooms I was thought to be capable of doing service in the NAAFI (Navy Army and Air Force Institutes). My seventeen-year-old granddaughter once asked me, 'What did you do when your were my age, Gran?' What could I say? it has all gone now. I still remember the words of one elderly lady when she said, 'If there be a war things will never be the same again.' How right she was.

Rhoda Woodward

Brenda Kirkham outside the gate of Shilson's Cottage in Calthorpe Street, 1935.

The New House

It was May 1937, I was four years old and my sister was just a baby; and amidst all the celebrations for the coronation of King George VI, our parents were busy packing, ready to leave our rented house in Calthorpe Street and take us to a brand new semi that they were buying in Grange Road, for the princely sum of £495 with a twenty-five-year mortgage. It was to be our home for the next eight and a half years.

Everything was new – the paths, the road signs and the young trees with protective wire mesh cylinders round their trunks, which were planted at intervals along the grass verges on either side of the road. The low walls between the front gardens and the pavement were just the right height to sit on or walk along, and because they were built with new rough brick, they were the cause of many grazed legs.

Dad worked wonders with the new garden, spending hours on it and turning the bare patch into a riot of colour. Often he would be out there when it was almost dark, leaning on his spade and chatting to neighbours over the fence or to people who had stopped to admire the garden on their way passed. Mum was so proud of the house, with all its mod cons – gas, electricity and three taps over the kitchen sink, one for hot water, one for cold and the third for rainwater that was collected in a huge square tank situated on the roof of the single storey kitchen. The kitchen was small, so it was called a 'kitchenette'. The sink was a deep, white porcelain one with a wooden draining board and a cupboard beneath it housing the gas and electricity meters that had to be fed regularly with pennies and shillings. There was a gas boiler for the washing and a gas ring for boiling the kettle or saucepan, and I tried to avoid lighting either as they would suddenly light with a

Celebrations in Calthorpe Street for the Coronation of King George VI in 1937.

frightening pop when a match was put to them.

The bathroom was white, with black and white check lino on the floor and I have every reason to remember the white wall tiles, because one day, in a temper, I slammed the bedroom door very hard and all the tiles shot off the wall and landed in a heap on the bathroom floor! However, our builder uncle came and repaired the damage.

In the front room downstairs, there was a tiled fireplace with a clock and small ornaments decorating its mantelpiece and, in the bay window, there stood a big square radiogram. If we dared to lift the top lid we could see the turntable and a little tin with gramophone needles inside. The lid of the

The view from the garden of houses along Grange Road in 1938.

cabinet was faded and the veneer crazed, except for a round, smooth, shiny patch protected from the sun by a potted fern standing on an embroidered mat. I cannot remember a sound of any kind being produced by that piece of furniture; maybe its role in life was just to be there for the fern! The room was only used when we had special visitors and then the fire was lit and everything dusted and polished, and as there was no table in there, it really was the 'sitting room'.

Two of the bedrooms had fireplaces and I remember one of them being used when as children we had to stay in bed because we were covered with measles or chickenpox spots and the weather was cold. The other bedroom grate had a fire in it on the special occasion when our brother was born, on a cold March morning and Mum had to stay in bed for almost a week, as was the rule for new mothers at that time.

The living room had a Triplex grate, black with red tiles, with a useless oven at the side that Mum said didn't even get hot enough to cook a rice pudding, so she used it to air freshly washed items that were needed in a hurry, such as vests and school socks, and nappies for our baby brother. Then one day the Triplex hit back and scorched the washing very badly, even though the oven door was open a crack.

The boiler for the hot water was behind the fire and the pipes went under the floor in our bedroom, making the lino warm to step out on to. When we had more of a blaze in winter, the water would boil in the tank with bubbling and banging noises and the taps had to be turned on to cool things down. Sometimes the chimney caught fire, much to Mum's alarm, and she would panic, shouting 'Damp it down, damp it down'. Next day she would be on her knees with the brush with the long wire handle, brushing soot from round the sides of the oven and as much as she could reach from up the chimney. Usually before things got to that state, Mum and a couple of neighbours arranged to have their chimneys done on the same day, then the sweep was sent for and he arrived on his bike, very early, usually on a spring morning, with rods and brushes tied in a bundle. Chimney sweeping was a messy procedure, so most things were moved out of the room or covered with old sheets. As children, our job was to stand outside and shout when the brush appeared out of the top of the chimney. The soot was put in a sack and kept, to be used months later in the garden. Cleaning up the house afterwards took all day, as everything had to be washed or wiped clean and that sooty, soapy-water smell seemed to hang around for ages. The house also felt cold and damp because the fire had been out so long, and it was always cold meat and potatoes for dinner!

The coal and fire-lighting sticks were kept in the 'coal hole'; this was a space under the stairs accessed via a small outside door in the side wall of the house. It was a dark, cobwebby place with a heap of slag one end, which, we were told, 'will be made into briquettes one day'. There were big lumps of coal that had to be smashed with the coal hammer into manageable-sized pieces that sometimes had patches of 'gold' on them. As we had to go outside to the coal hole, it was a place we dreaded visiting in winter when it was cold, dark and raining, but if the scuttle needed to be filled, the job was done as quickly as possible with an old mac around the shoulders, a shovel in one

hand and a torch in the other and a fervent hope not to come across any spiders.

Our third bedroom was very tiny and was called 'the box room' but when the war started, it was turned into a bedroom with just a single bed, a small dressing table that was so close to the bed it was a job to open the drawers, and a minute wardrobe. This tiny room was occupied by a succession of WAAFs for the next five years. They were girls who worked for the MAP (Ministry of Aircraft Production) in Southam Road in Banbury. One was an Edinburgh girl, called Margaret, whose birthday was 3 September – not a happy date! She was my favourite of

Reg and Dorothy Tew with their daughters Brenda and Gillian (seated on her mother's knee). This picture was taken by Reg as an experiment into delayed exposure on his new camera.

all the girls who stayed with us over the years, not just because we loved to stroke the fur coat she had hanging on a hook behind the bedroom door, but mainly because she had a grown-up's bike that she let me ride, standing on the pedals, down to the island and back.

Almost every house on the estate contained children, who were either resident or evacuees from London or other cities that were being bombed. There were children everywhere, the schools were full and we were never short of friends or someone to fall out with! We played in the roads as there were almost no cars and only an occasional delivery vehicle, such as the railway lorry bringing parcels, Hobbs the oil-man, selling paraffin, doormats, lino squares and other household necessities, or the greengrocer with his horse and cart, bringing fruit and vegetables, that he delivered to each house in a basket that he carried on a hook that he had instead of a hand. The horse meanwhile walked slowly and automatically along the road, grazing on the edge of the grass verges as it went.

The families in the new houses in 1937 were still there in 1945, because no one moved house during those war years, so we all knew everyone. Salt Lane was our playground in summer; we made dens in the hedges and ditches and climbed the trees and we knew exactly where to find the first violets and catkins. The boys climbed higher up the trees than we girls dared to and they tied thick ropes to branches for swings. We annoyed the farmer by playing in the corn field and we walked to Cherry's Mill to fish in the brook with our home-made fishing rods, baited with bread rolled into balls or worms that we had dug out of our garden. In the evenings, we had to collect huge bunches of dandelion leaves and keck to feed the rabbits that Dad had in hutches in our garden and we shed many a tear over the demise of these animals, when they went to augment someone's meat ration. My sister was inconsolable when a little rabbit that she had been told was hers as a pet, vanished never to be seen again. She still feels cheated to this day.

The 'Dig for Victory' campaign caused our lawn to be replaced with potatoes and in place of flowerbeds, there were cabbages and sprouts that released clouds of white butterflies as we walked past. The greenhouse was full of tomato plants, dosed regularly with liquid from a tank full of sheep 'daggings' and water. They were the tastiest tomatoes ever!

Gillian Kirkham with Peter, a playmate who lived in Addison Road.

We walked to school, clean and tidy, in groups each morning, then walked home at midday for our dinner, then back to school for two o'clock and at four o'clock another walk home. By this time we were not looking quite so tidy and our shoes were scuffed from clambering on the hospital wall, that had a nice flat top where the railings had been taken away for the war effort. Sometimes I had fourpence halfpenny tied into the corner of my hanky, to buy a large loaf from England's the bakers in South Bar on my way home. I must confess that because bread was never wrapped, the loaf had quite a large 'recess' at one end by the time it was handed over to Mum!

We watched lorries with long trailers loaded with crashed planes travelling along Oxford Road and soldiers driving tanks that ploughed across the grass verges as they misjudged the corners; and American servicemen asked if we had older sisters, but the war itself seemed a long way away. We worried of course, because we could see our parents were worried, especially when we heard the planes going over to bomb Coventry and the sky lit up. We had an air-raid shelter in the garden, but we only used it a couple of times. We waved to convoys of lorries packed with soldiers as they drove slowly past, then we ran home to listen to *Children's Hour* without any idea where all those men were going.

Then in 1945 everything changed. The war ended with VE Day in May and VJ Day in August, the evacuees had gone home and some folk began thinking of moving away from Banbury. One of these was our dad; he had always dreamed of having a farm of his own, so with the war over he set about searching for one that was right for us and after weeks of studying the adverts in the *Farmers Weekly* and *Farmer and Stockbreeder* and going by train all over the country to view places, he chose one in Devon. Three weeks before Christmas we left the house in Grange Road and said goodbye to our friends with many hugs and tears and promises to write often and set off for a completely strange, new life – but that is another story.

Brenda Kirkham

CHAPTER 3

War Years Remembered

Bill Hindle with his regiment under canvas. This photograph was probably taken in India; Bill is red second from the right.

Bill and Enid on their wedding day, Boxing Day 1937.

The Can

Born and raised in Bishop Auckland, County Durham, Bill Hindle joined the Army in the early 1930s to escape the Depression, which had had such a devastating effect on job prospects in the North East. His unit, a cavalry regiment, was soon posted to India, which at the time was the training ground for most of the British Army. In 1935 the Army discharged many of its regular soldiers, shipping them back to England for demobilization into reserve battalions. On arrival at Southampton, Bill was given a choice of destinations for his rail warrant; knowing full well that his chances of finding work in his home town were little better than when he had left to join the Army, Bill decided to try his luck in London.

He never made it to London. Stopping instead at Banbury he stepped down onto the platform at 10.30 p.m. and looked around the almost deserted station for a friendly face. Needing a bed for the night he approached a porter who remembered that Jack Keen, a shunter for Great Western Railway, was looking for a paying lodger and directed him to Gibbs Road in Grimsbury; the rest, as they say, is history. Jack's youngest daughter Enid soon fell head over heels in love with Bill who was equally smitten, and soon after he had secured a job with the Northern Aluminium Company (Alcan), in their newly opened Southam Road factory, Bill and Enid were married. Their honeymoon was to be short-lived, however, and at the outbreak of the Second World War Bill, as a reservist, was among the first to be called up, joining his now mechanized cavalry regiment with the rank of Staff Sergeant based on his previous

Top left and right: *Precious days! Bill's last leave before going overseas.*

Bill and Enid with Bill's sister-in-law (on his left) just before the start of the Second World War in 1939.

service. He was soon sent overseas and, like many others, Enid was left to endure the anguish of his absence for many long wartime years.

How could the can that dominated the top shelf of my grandmother's larder be so important? Why couldn't we just open it up and eat the contents, after all everything else in there was for eating wasn't it? To this small boy it didn't make sense. Enwrapped in a brightly coloured label showing pictures of luscious fruits in shades of red, the black and gold lettering seductively implied the contents to be exotic and succulent – a feast fit only for the gods – in my youthful imagination! It was wartime and food had become scarce – especially products from other countries. The years passed and the contents of the larder slowly diminished until, eventually, the top shelf had only one occupant.

My Uncle Bill had marched off to war in 1939, and his wife, my Auntie Enid, moved in next door to us to stay with my grandparents 'for the duration', which, although we didn't realize it then, was to be for quite a long time. Apparently Uncle Bill was very partial to tinned tomatoes and the can, I was told in no uncertain terms, was to be opened only upon his safe return. With everything being rationed it was unlikely that a replacement would ever be found so there it must stay. I resigned myself to the fact that these forbidden fruits would only be consumed on a very special occasion. But my curiosity lingered, and from time to time I would gaze wistfully at the top shelf, noting the traces of rust which were beginning to appear around the rim of the can, and longed for the day when Uncle Bill would return to enjoy his treat.

One day, on my way home from school, I was met by an almost delirious Auntie Enid. Hardly able to contain her excitement she

Home at last: Bill and Enid reunited!

told me that our hero was coming in on the very next train and that she and I were going to the station to meet him. What a homecoming that was! He had been away for almost five years and as a tank commander in the Eighth Army he had fought in the desert at El Alamein, taken part in the invasion of Italy, and was one of the first British troops to enter Berlin after the Nazis' capitulation. Through his letters and the newspapers we had followed his exploits for so long, and here at last, he was home with us – safe and sound!

From then on I spent every possible moment in my grandparents' front room, which had become Enid and Bill's 'love nest'. I realize now what a nuisance I must have been and how they must have wished this inquisitive little boy would leave them to make up for all those years of separation. Thinking back they must have cursed my presence many, many times as I questioned him on his exploits, hanging on his every word and marvelling at his souvenirs of the war: the silver-sheathed dress dagger and epaulettes (taken from a high-ranking German officer no less!) and, as I counted out the colourful, high-denomination (and quite worthless!) pre-war German banknotes on the floor, I would fancy myself to be a 'millionaire'.

However, such is the callowness of youth that in all the excitement of his return I completely forgot about the ubiquitous can of tomatoes and it was not until many years later, after Uncle Bill had died, that I was to hear the end of the story. Reminiscing one day with Auntie Enid in the British Legion Home where she spent her last days, I asked her if Uncle Bill had enjoyed his tomatoes and whether he realized just how long they had been sitting on the shelf. She told me that when they arrived home from the station on that fateful day she had cooked his favourite meal of eggs, bacon, mushrooms and of course the tomatoes, just as she had rehearsed in her imagination so many times during those long, anxious years. Proudly and lovingly she placed it on the table before him whereupon he broke down and wept. Overwhelmed with the emotion of the homecoming it had been just too much for him to bear and he was unable to eat a thing!

I have pondered this many times since and have come to the conclusion that the saga of the tomatoes had after all come to a fitting end. They had served their purpose well. While they were up there on the shelf they had kept alive our belief in his safe return. For them to have been merely eaten would have been an ignominious end for this icon of faith that had sustained us for so long.

John Neville

War Games

I walked through the park the other day and went out of the gate past the children's swings. I glanced to my left, saw the laurel bushes fronting Bath Road and the bottom of Queens Road, and my mind flew back sixty years and the laurel bushes changed into our fighting aircraft.

One bush in particular had a big branch growing from the ground at an angle of about 15 degrees and was strong enough to take the weight of a small boy sitting on the end; this was the 'rear turret'. From here my four machine guns, which never ran out of ammo, could command most of Queens Road, Bath Road and the car park. Any

Number 22 Bath Road, where Alan Sargeant spent his childhood from 1938 to 1952.

enemy aircraft attacking the Co-op at the top of Queens Road would be within range – after all, if the shop were destroyed how could I give Mrs Stevens our ration books and repeat parrot-fashion 'twenty-two eighty-seven'? Closer to me at the bottom of the street there were the families of all my mates to protect. Had the imaginary bits of Luftwaffe planes been real, their mums would have been sweeping mashed Messerschmitt, strips of Stuka, hunks of Heinkel, dollops of Dornier and blobs of Blohm & Voss off their front steps.

The branch was also low enough to 'bale out' onto the grass below without hurting yourself. But real parachuting had to be done from the sandstone wall at the side of the gate. It was about six feet tall and we used to jump off it onto the grass below. 'Feet together, roll over on your side', we

knew all the parachute drill. A sharp smack in the stomach on the harness release and the imaginary parachute fell off, leaving us airborne commandos ready to go into action. A quick dash across the disused bowling green (now a garden) bayoneting a few enemy on the way and we were in the cover of the forest within striking distance of Gestapo headquarters. Somebody had very cleverly camouflaged it as Neithrop House where the school dentist and 'Nitty' Nora the school nurse ran their 'torture chamber'.

We never dared emerge from the forest but we could give the defending garrison in the imaginary trench (which just happened to be the path) a good hammering. Hard pieces of clay from the garden between the wall and the bowling green made very good hand grenades because when they were thrown onto hard surfaces they burst and spread in what we thought was a very realistic way. Some of us wore short jackets with elastic waistbands, which was ideal for carrying this type of ammo. The head of the Gestapo was also heavily disguised, as 'Scabby' Rawlings the park keeper. He was constantly on the prowl and had to be avoided at all costs as he was not best pleased with us for making a mess on the paths. In addition to our Mills bombs we all carried knives, catapults and/or peashooters, plus any bit of stick for a rifle. Somebody made a kind of wooden gun based on a football rattle that sounded like a Tommy gun when you turned the handle.

In those days there was a stream in the park which we used to play in for hours. Although clothes were rationed, small boys still got them dirty in no time flat and at that time there were no washing machines; our one concession to clothes rationing was taking off our boots before wading up the 'Chindwin' to get to the 'Japs' who were in the jungle near the toilets on Warwick Road. We had to move very quietly and keep our rifles above our heads although the water only came up to our calves. A word on boots: boys' boots were always like black leather Army boots with steel studs and 'segs', and we used to get a clip round the ear from a parent (anybody's parent) if we ran and slid along the path to make sparks come off our feet. The more affluent boys wore shoes.

Occasionally the LDV (Local Defence Volunteers, later the Home Guard, or 'Dad's Army') would have exercises in the park; if they had been issued with blank ammo it was exciting to here the bangs. We used to sit on the park wall and criticize their infantry tactics and we thought that, compared with us, they were useless at

remaining hidden (ah, the wisdom of seven-year-old hardened veterans).

All hostilities ceased at teatime when it was time to go home and be scrubbed clean in cold water with carbolic soap (rationed) before being allowed to sit at the table. To my Grandmother my hands were always 'like pigs' backs'.

Twenty years later I became friends with a young cabinet maker from Berlin who had come to work at Henry Stones' under the Young Workers' Exchange Scheme. He couldn't speak much English and I was learning German. He told me that the kids in Berlin used to play just the same, only with the names changed round.

In the Second World War the firm Dornier used to make the infamous pencil-thin bombers but the last time I saw the name was on the side of a large white vehicle parked outside the Nuffield hospital in Oxford. This time Dornier's equipment bombarded me with ultra-sound, making a surgical operation unnecessary. Some swords have been turned into ploughshares and some grubby, bloodthirsty little boys have grown into old men.

Alan Sargeant

Grimsbury Boy

Born in the 1930s, I grew up during the Second World War. With the austerity and the shortages that prevailed, you might think that this was a rather less than idyllic period for boys to be growing up but in fact it was the most exciting of times. The war provided us with many heroes and our imaginations were continually being fired by their exploits, which we followed avidly in the newspapers. We were able to identify any aircraft and could point out the differences between a Hawker Hurricane and a Spitfire or a Lancaster and a Wellington at a glance. I would spend hours drawing pictures of aeroplanes, filling in every tiny detail. My dad would make wooden models for me and I remember the excitement of finding in my stocking one Christmas morning a silver Lockheed Lightning fighter-bomber, complete with its American insignia painstakingly painted on its fuselage and twin tail plane.

Rationing

Food rationing was a constant worry and queuing outside shops for even the most basic items became the order of the day for our mothers. 'Dig for Victory' was one of the slogans of the times as the government exhorted everyone to cultivate as much ground as possible to supplement the ever-decreasing food supplies. Fruit and vegetables were grown in back gardens and allotments and all in all we ate well. By today's standards, we enjoyed a very healthy diet – at least everything then was 'organic'. My grandfather and my dad had adjoining plots in the allotments at the end of Gibbs Road (now Grimsbury Drive), and would vie with one another to see who could produce the biggest marrow or the best row of peas. Because of the shortages nothing was wasted. On Mondays we always had 'bubble and squeak', a concoction made up from Sunday's leftovers. One of my favourites was 'dried egg' – reconstituted egg processed and packaged in America – which, when mixed with water and cooked, resembled scrambled eggs. It could also be used in recipes as a substitute for fresh eggs. The BBC dedicated radio programmes to providing recipes for housewives, offering

John Neville with Scottie the dog in the summer of 1939, weeks before the outbreak of the Second World War.

advice on how to make do with whatever came to hand – at mealtimes you literally took potluck! My mother was not a particularly imaginative cook but I could always rely on my grandmother for special treats. I would walk into town to fetch her brewer's yeast from Mr Ayres' shop in Church Lane and as a reward she would put a small cottage loaf on her baking tray especially for me – I can still recall the smell of bread, left to rise under a pristine white tea cloth on the hearth in front of the fire. I remember too the taste of the yeast, which I would pick at on my way home; rolling it into pellets and letting it dissolve and fizz on my tongue.

Radio

In those days I spent as much time in my grandparents' house as I did in our own and

I never tired of listening to my ex-railwayman grandfather's jokes and anecdotes. My father was a bit of a radio buff and he would make crystal sets out of pieces of wire and something called a 'cat's whisker'. These would be mounted on a board and attached to headphones; we would then take turns at twiddling the knobs to find a station being broadcast. Dad's pride and joy was the 'Alba' radiogram, which almost filled our tiny living room. I grew up listening to the strains of music played by Roy Fox and his Orchestra and singers such as Al Bowley and Rudy Vallee from Dad's pre-war 78rpm gramophone records. These fragile discs had to be religiously wiped clean with a soft cloth after each recital before being carefully put back into their brown cardboard sleeves. Wireless programmes such as Tommy Handley's *ITMA* (It's That Man Again) and *Henry Hall's Guest Night* were obligatory listening throughout the war years; later on of course we had *Dick Barton Special Agent*, *Saturday Night Theatre* and *In Town Tonight* to look forward to. To save my grandparents the expense of buying a radio for themselves, Dad rigged up a cable that stretched between the two houses, connecting our radiogram to a loud speaker in their house; thanks to his ingenuity this meant that they could listen to any programme we chose. I don't think they minded too much, at least I never heard them complain!

Evacuees

One of the earliest recollections I have of the war's disruption to our family life was of an evacuee named Hubert arriving one day on our doorstep. Much older than me, he had come to Banbury along with other children, refugees from the blitzed East End of London. My only lasting memory of him was that his mother, who visited us most weekends, brought him presents of sweets, chocolate and toys the like of which I had never seen, but as he didn't share any of these goodies with me I soon lost interest in Hubert and to my relief, he eventually moved on. Normality in our small household was short-lived, however. After being bombed out of their house in Beckingham in Kent, my Uncle Syd, Auntie Dora and Cousin Jennifer descended upon us and, although we didn't know it then, they were to stay until almost the end of the war. Our tiny house was full to overflowing, with four grown-ups and three children under the one roof which meant the loss of my own room for the duration – a sacrifice, I consoled myself, that was my contribution to the war effort!

Not withstanding the war, as a member of an extended family and being surrounded by aunts, who all lived nearby, I was subjected to close scrutiny at all times. I had to be scrubbed and in bed by seven o'clock in the evening, even at weekends, whilst my pals would be allowed out to play until all hours. But it all changed when my sister Elizabeth was born. Suddenly the focus of attention was shifted from me onto the new baby. Freedom at last! Now I could stay out from morning until quite late during the long, double summertime days and no one seemed to notice how late it got. Throughout the school holidays and at weekends our gang would roam the surrounding countryside in search of adventure. There was always plenty to do, whether it was kicking or throwing a ball, or acting out our fantasies as Robin Hood and his Merry Men or as commandos crawling up on an unsuspecting enemy. There were bonfires to be lit, camps to be built, and rivers to be swum – we were never short of ideas; and never bored – there weren't enough hours in the day! In the absence of the shop-bought, sophisticated toys so prevalent today, we improvised. Bows and arrows, fashioned from willow branches cut from the osier beds next to the canal, made perfect weapons, and should the game of the day require such things as swords or guns they were easily fashioned from pieces of wood and scrap metal pipe – our imaginations did the rest. Catapults were obligatory; the frame had to be cut from a carefully selected forked branch and special heavy-gauge elastic purchased from Robins the ironmongers in the Market Place – the pouch was made of soft leather tongue cut from an old shoe. In this wartime atmosphere it didn't seem out of place to be living out the violent exploits of our heroes, albeit in play. Nowadays our 'war games' would probably be frowned upon as being politically incorrect. An old, almost submerged, waterlogged punt wallowing in the river behind Grimsbury Mill became a pirate ship or, on a hot summer's day, it was a perfect diving board to launch us into the Cherwell's cool water. In this *Just William* world our mischief rarely extended beyond occasional scrumping expeditions into neighbours gardens and orchards, or knocking on doors and running away.

The changing seasons called for different kinds of activity. A favourite spot all the year round was the Brickle, a pond situated in the middle of the field behind the Blacklocks Hotel. In the summer newts and sticklebacks were there to be caught and carried home in jam jars. In the winter as soon as it froze over we became ice hockey players, using walking sticks smuggled from the house. More often than not someone would end up running home wet through after falling through the ice. Cuts and bruises were commonplace and

were displayed as badges of courage in the presence of our contemporaries – 'big boys didn't cry'. There were seasons too for games such as whip and top, marbles, conkers and the like, all played in the almost traffic-free streets. During the war only vehicles needed for official business were seen on the roads. These had to be modified to save vital fuel stocks and we thought it very funny to see a billowing bag of gas perched on the top of a small saloon car, looking for all the world like a galleon in full sail! Buses towed small trailers which, presumably, contained some kind of fuel-saving device; these proved to be too much of a challenge for some of the older lads who would sometimes jump onto the back of the trailers and cling on as they pulled away from the bus stop, seeing who could stay on the longest. Many a grazed knee resulted from this dangerous exploit but I don't recall anything more serious happening to any of them.

Another reminder that it was wartime came with the systematic removal of all the iron railings and gates from outside every house. I remember being puzzled as to what possible use they would be put to help win the war. I came to the conclusion that things must be going pretty badly for us if they needed to use our spiked railings as spears to repel the foe! I must have been contemplating this possibility when, standing too close while they cut down our railings, a piece of heavy iron work dropped onto my foot, it was extremely painful and eventually, one by one, I lost all the toenails! I have since discovered that instead of helping the war effort the railings were dumped when it was discovered that they were unsuitable for melting down.

Yanks

For a time even going to school was an adventure. Attending Grimsbury Council School and living in Gibbs Road meant that

I had to walk to school along East Street every school day. The Blacklocks Hotel and the field behind it had been turned into a barracks for troops awaiting embarkation and whilst other regiments had passed through the camp, in 1944 it was the turn of the American GIs to take up residence – what excitement! We soon became streetwise where the Yanks were concerned and 'Got any gum, chum?' was a familiar cry as we hung around the East Street entrance. We all acquired sisters – real or imaginary – and played mercilessly on the Americans' gullibility, shamelessly spinning any yarn that might wheedle sweets or chocolate or better still, some item of GI kit from them. As a result we started turning up for school wearing all manner of US militaria – badges, forage caps and the like. It eventually reached such proportions that our headmaster, Norman Scroxton, had to put a ban on our unofficial 'uniforms'. Another strange phenomenon distinguished the Americans' presence. Each morning on our way to school we would see dozens of strange looking white rubber objects strewn around. After much speculation the general consensus amongst us younger kids was that they must be wrappers from something very special that the Yanks were keeping for themselves. I suppose, thinking about it now, that wasn't a bad guess! I have one especially vivid memory of the American soldier. I remember a very tall, somewhat dishevelled and unsteady figure in a flapping khaki greatcoat, standing on the railway bridge which connects Grimsbury to the town centre, somewhat worse for wear after a visit to the Talbot public house in the High Street. I can see him now hugging a large bag of sweets, he handed some to every passing child and I'd swear there were tears in his eyes – perhaps he was thinking of his own children back home. I can understand better now why so many of our sisters were so eager to become the 'GI brides' of these glamorous, charismatic and generous visitors who had come to us from across the sea.

Ghost Town

Then, almost overnight, they had decamped and were gone. We crowded the streets to watch the truckloads of troops pass by. All manner of vehicles rumbled through the town on their way to the costal ports and the ships that would take them over to France for the D-Day landings. For some time after they'd gone Banbury was like a ghost town. It is sad to realize that so many of them didn't return home to their families, but one thing is certain, they left behind some fond and lasting memories for the people of Grimsbury – and for one small boy in particular.

John Neville

CHAPTER 4
Relocation

From the 1960s onwards, Banbury experienced what could be said to be the beginning of the end of its small market town status as many factories and companies from cities such as London and Birmingham began to relocate here. With them came their employees, and also those in search of employment. The following pieces recount this transition and convey an image of Banbury as not only an expanding and changing town, but also a town in which many people entrusted their hopes, dreams and their futures.

Number 5 Merton Street, the house into which George Wilding and his family moved when they came down from Scotland in the early 1960s.

In Search of Work

My dad George Wilding came to Banbury in July 1962. He came here to get work as he had been out of work for two years where we lived in Scotland. We were, and are Salvationists, and Dad saw an advert in the Salvation Army paper in 1961 for work at the then Alcan factory in Southam Road. The advert said that they would also help with getting housing for families. Dad had to write to the officer in charge who was, at the time, Major John Elsworth. The bandsman who was responsible for finding housing was a Yorkshire man named Charlie Brown, who had also moved down to Banbury. Dad came down to Banbury in October 1961 but unfortunately was not successful in finding employment. The following June, however, he heard again that there was work available; this time it was for Automotive Products, a new firm that had just moved to Banbury. Dad got the job, and he came down on his own to work and find a house. In the meantime he lodged with Mr and Mrs Frank Laird who later became my father and mother-in-law. My mum came down from Scotland in August to help Dad look for a house, and they found one in Merton Street, at No. 5. The house was opposite what used to be the cattle market, and there was another row of houses on the opposite side of the street, further along, which is now the site of a Muslim mosque. There was Mum, Dad, my sister Morag, my younger brother George and myself. My eldest brother, Arthur, who was married to Molly and had a little girl called Christine in 1963 and later Lynn, also moved to Banbury in 1963 where he too went to work at Automotive Products. I was fifteen when we first came to Banbury and my husband's grandmother got me a job at Bernard Smith's in Parsons Street, from there I went to the Postiche where they made wigs as they still do today.

Banbury has changed a great deal since then. Where Debenhams is now there was a road through to Castle Street and another row of houses. Our Salvation Army hall has changed a lot also: while the outside remains the same, the inside does not. Inside the door there used to be a small foyer with stairs on either side leading up to a gallery, but now we have a lovely suite of halls with our main worship hall upstairs and junior hall downstairs. We also have other smaller rooms and an office. We used to have open-airs at the Cross on a Saturday and Sunday evening when we first came. At this time the coaches used to stop for a break in the summer as they were travelling through the town, and we used to get a lot of people who liked to hear the band and enjoy the singing. When the motorway opened this stopped a lot of coaches coming into the town, and with the declining number in the band our open-airs ceased. In the early sixties there was no shopping centres at all in Banbury, only High Street shops, Market Place, Church Lane and Parsons Street. The first centre (the Castle Shopping Centre) was built after I had married and started to have my children, and the second (the Castle Quay Shopping Centre), only last year.

Evelyn Laird

The One Hundredth Family

On 14 August 1964 the Banbury Guardian *reported on the first family to move to Banbury from Birmingham in preparation for* the completion of the new Bird's factory. They were Ted Connor, his wife Cathy, and their one-year-old daughter Catherine, who moved into a newly built house in Edmunds Road. Three weeks later in the 3 September edition of the Banbury Guardian the headline 'Birds First Century' appeared; this piece relates to this migration.

The one hundredth family to move into the Banbury area on the gradual transfer of employees of General Foods Workers from Birmingham occurred on 31 August 1964 when Bill Marshall – at the time a coffee roaster operator in the Bradford Street factory – moved into a four-bedroomed council house at No. 7 Chepstow Gardens on Bretch Hill. With him were his wife Sylvia and their four daughters, Petula (aged eleven), Heather (nine), Dawn (six) and eight-month-old Cheryl, together with the family pet Dachshund and two of her puppies. The event was recorded in both the Banbury Guardian and the now defunct Banbury Gazette, together with photographs of the family being presented with a large bouquet of flowers.

At the time the Banbury factory was still in the process of being erected and it was at least two more years before it was in 'full flow' as a production unit. This meant that a fair number of employees had to be shuttled between Banbury and Birmingham every day by bus (supplied of course by the firm). This made for a long day – especially for those on twelve-hour shifts!

June and Trevor Curtis in 1975 with their sons Lee and baby Andrew.

Bill retired in 1989 after thirty-one years of service, and all his daughters have married – three in Banbury and one in Sibford – so the move must have been a success for them.

Cheryl Gilbert

Londoners

I moved to Banbury from London in 1970 with my husband Trevor as part of his firm's relocation programme. We weren't the only family; I think there were at least twenty others and most of us were given houses on the new Ruscote Estate. At the time the estate wasn't finished and Woodfield, where we lived, was the last road of completed houses; the rest was just a building site!

In the early seventies it could be said that Banbury was still a relatively small market town and this was quite a shock for us as we were used to being near to the centre of London where we could have access to all the shops and theatres. Stranger still, there was a farm at the top of our road and through the night you could hear the cattle mooing. This was eerie, and very alien to us as we were more accustomed to hearing the sounds of the city.

Despite the strangeness of life in Banbury compared to our former lives in London, I remember during our first week here, which was the week of the Banbury Fair, how great it was to have a fair in the centre of town! This I'd never seen, as fairs in London were always in parks or on commons. The fair even had a boxing booth, although that stopped after a few years.

When we first moved to Banbury we were very homesick and went back to London at every opportunity, but after a while we managed to adapt. I think this was helped by the fact that it was so easy to make friends, as most of the people on our estate had moved either from London or Birmingham, so we were all new together.

We have lived in Banbury for thirty years now and I couldn't imagine living anywhere else. We have watched it develop from a small market town to the rapidly growing industrial and retail centre that it is today. The pace of life in Banbury has changed over the years, but I suppose that is inevitable with all the changes the town has seen.

June Curtis

A Stranger's Anecdote

I first came to Banbury in October 1962, to become employed by the Hunt Edmunds Brewery, which was opposite the Town Hall in Bridge Street. As a 'country boy' from Wiltshire I was glad to escape from the claustrophobic and cosmopolitan atmosphere of Coventry, where I was previously employed.

Banbury in 1962 was still the small 'sleepy' agricultural town it had been for centuries and was only just beginning to change into the place we now know. Plans were afoot, a few years later, to build a vast new complex of council housing (now the Ruscote area) to replace those in the town. The majority of town dwellers lived in the Cherwell District (that area bounded by Bridge

John and Minnie Saville pictured with their grandson Lee during the mid-1970s.

Street, Broad Street, George Street and Lower Cherwell Street) in which the Hunt Edmunds Brewery was situated. Hundreds of Banbury folk were born, lived and died in this 'working-class' enclave, which has now been demolished.

I soon came to experience the territorial pride exhibited by those with whom I worked. For instance those born in Grimsbury were not Banburians (neither did they wish to be). To be living

in Broad Street was in some way superior to having been brought up in Canal Street. To me, this Cherwell area was a hub of activity and respectability, where everyone knew everyone else (and all about them too!). To live in George Street, Upper or Lower Windsor Street, Upper or Lower Cherwell Streets, together with others, was a source of pride and identification. I experienced an air of co-operation and belonging, mingled

Hunt Edmunds Brewery, Bridge Street, Banbury.

with an extreme independence and radicalism, which appeared in-born in a true Banburian. I came to love and respect the local inhabitants for this, and soon acclimatized to my new surroundings.

At first sight the Hunt Edmunds Brewery appeared to be an archaic, paternalistic place of employment. This it was, in various aspects, but the firm also had an atmosphere of 'belonging' – something I had not before experienced. I am still convinced that the employees were not attracted by their lowly weekly wage, but because they looked forward to seeing and being with their fellow Banburians each day. Paternalistic it

surely was, and any employee could approach the company chairman (who attended daily) personally to be heard and listened to with respect.

Having renounced the hurly-burly of city life, the introduction to my brewery colleagues is still a vivid memory. As I was introduced to the first, a lovely black Labrador dog issued from beneath his desk, wagging is tail in welcome. I was asked, quite seriously whether I would like 'a pint' – at nine o'clock in the morning! I was forced to decline, and soon learned that a 'drink' was not a cup of tea!

Much later I was told a story by an employee concerning this gentleman (for

Hunt Edmunds Brewery, January 1963. These workers had been out clearing the snow in the yard. From left to right: David Williams, Alf Hone, Frank Cross, 'Daggle' Mold.

that he genuinely was), which was probably apocryphal. Apparently all breweries keep cats in the brewhouse to restrict the rodents attracted by the copious amounts of barley grain used. Hunt Edmunds certainly had their full complement of cats.

The brewing 'tuns' containing grain, hops and hot water were cylindrically upright in shape, having circular wooden lids at the top, which are hinged across their diameter. These lids were usually only half-closed during the brewing process and the brewery cats found them a dry warm place on which to sleep. During one brew, a poor sleeping cat must have rolled over and fallen into the boiling mass below. Much later, its body was discovered and duly reported to my colleague, whereupon he enquired which

cat it was. 'He was the black one, wasn't he?' he asked. On this being confirmed he told his staff to carry on as normal because, he said, 'we were only brewing mild ale in that tun'. Mild ale is darker in colour (and cheaper) than the more popular bitter ale and the cat's demise could not have affected the colour of the brew!

A true tale of the Hunt Edmunds Brewery concerns the company chairman's car. It was a sleek Alvis saloon in metallic grey – a somewhat costly and rare car. An elderly ex-drayman was employed solely to wash and polish the Alvis every day. This he dutifully did, until one day he reported that the car had 'changed colour', and looked awful. The cleaning rags were found to be completely grey – the original colour of the car.

An investigation was launched, and it transpired that the unfortunate cleaner had been issued with a very abrasive brand of 'polish' which should never have been used on such a car. Needless to say the car had to be resprayed by the Alvis Company in Coventry and the Hunt Edmunds Brewery Chairman saw the lighter side of the inconvenience he was caused. To this day I wonder whether the 'wrong' polish issued was deliberate or not! However, the cleaner carried on as normal, but given the suitable polish advised by the makers of the car.

Of the physical character of the town in 1962, little is left as it forges on into a new millennium. As an 'alien' in the town, I consider it a privilege to have known it and its work people. One can only trust that the new guardians of the town will be imbued with the same independence and radicalism, which was the hallmark of their forbears.

David Williams

CHAPTER 5
First Jobs

Looking down on Banbury Cross and the High Street, where Messrs Stockton Sons & Fortescue had their firm of solicitors. As an office boy for the firm in 1949, fourteen-year-old Alan Sargeant had to walk the town centre streets of Banbury, hand-delivering mail and collecting 'feof-farm rents'. (Supplied by Martin Blinkhorn)

The Office Boy

I started my first job at the age of fifteen in 1949. I was a pupil at Dashwood Road School and shortly before I left I was called into the headmaster's office where Mr Proctor told me that a firm of solicitors, Messrs Stockton, Sons & Fortescue of No. 38 High Street, Banbury, were looking for an office boy and that he had arranged an interview for me. I duly attended and was shown up three or four flight of stairs to a small attic room where I was interviewed by two ladies, one of whom told me that the 'honorarium' would be 12s 6d per week. (Note that *Kelly's Directory* of Banbury cost 7s 6d in those days.) For that princely sum I would have to arrive at work at 8.30 in the morning, light the fires, dust some of the desks, bring in and sort the incoming mail and look after the outgoing mail. Finishing time in the evening was 5.30 provided that I was not needed to take any late mail to the post office on the opposite side of the High Street. I was aghast at this for a full week's work because at the time I was working as a paper boy for Bill Gilkes the newsagent at the top of Parsons Street who gave me fifteen bob a week for delivering his Warwick Road round which started at the old police station and finished at the Barley Mow, and only took a couple of hours in the morning. However, I deluded myself that this was for a trial period and accepted. When I started a few weeks later I felt as though I was entering a time machine. I was shown to a high desk with a climb-up stool, which looked like a relic from an old Victorian counting house. There was a six-inch high black wooden balustrade surrounding the back half and leaning up against it was a small black rectangular wooden plaque with these words in gold lettering:

WORK HARD FOR NINE HOURS A DAY AND DON'T WORRY THEN ONE DAY YOU MAY BECOME A BOSS AND WORK FOR EIGHTEEN HOURS A DAY AND HAVE ALL THE WORRY!

On the wall facing me was a portrait of an old Victorian gentleman holding a top hat. I was told that this was Mr Munton, from the time, 100 years earlier, when the firm was called Munton and Stockton. Standing on the mantelpiece below the portrait were a hand-grenade and an artillery shell from the First World War. At my left elbow was an early plug-type telephone exchange with 'eyelids' which closed when someone was ringing the switchboard. I was told that I would be shown how to use it but first I had to be introduced to the other members of the firm. The form was to refer to all people as Mr, Mrs or Miss followed sometimes by their Christian name and sometimes by their surname. So there were Mr Claude (Fortescue), Mr Arthur (Stockton), Miss Ensor and, a few weeks after I started there, Mr Huntriss. The gentlemen partners were always addressed as 'Sir' and Miss Ensor as 'Miss'; other senior members of staff were always addressed as Mr Lowe, Mr Ward, etc. The whole atmosphere of the place was of another age, the people were generally very polite to one another, like in the television series *Upstairs, Downstairs*. Mr Ward, however, was of a somewhat brusquer nature – he never referred to me as Alan; to him I was always 'boy'! Introductions over, I was sent for by Mr Lowe the book-keeper. He gave me 15s and a small notebook and told me that I was to buy stamps for the firm's postage out of the 15s and record it very carefully in the note book. In those days the office boy delivered the local mail, and a

A slightly earlier view of the High Street, looking up towards Banbury Cross. Calthorpe Street winds round in the left of the picture, where most of the buildings pictured have now been demolished. The road is now mostly dedicated to car parking space. At the top of the picture it is clear how close the fields came to the town centre; they have since been built over as the town has expanded. (Supplied by Martin Blinkhorn)

first class stamp only cost 2d. Mr Lowe was very particular about his ledger; before making an entry he would select a pen and try the entry on a piece of scrap paper. When he was satisfied that the pen worked properly he would approach the tall lectern upon which rested the revered volume, make the entry above his round ebony ruler and blot it with a semi-circular blotting paper roller. In later years when I was a draughtsman I saw some superb pen work but nothing that impressed me as much as the beautiful

uniformity of Mr Lowe's ledger.

On my first morning an older boy took me on the daily round to deliver letters by hand to clients and other solicitors in the town. We went down the High Street first to No. 35 where old Mr Lamley-Fisher practised on his own, then over the road to Aplin, Hunt & Thomas next to the old post office, and then back across the road to Whitehornes & Haines who were near S.H. Jones the wine merchants, and finally down to the offices of Fairfax-Barfield at No. 29 Bridge Street next to the Catherine

Wheel pub near the Town Hall; their office boy was Mr Alan Olds who retired recently from Aplins in West Bar.

On my second morning I was inducted into the routine of fire-lighting. There were four grates, which had to be emptied of ashes at 8.30 each morning and the fires re-laid and lit. This involved going down to the cellar, which was lit from a skylight (since blocked up), and chopping logs into kindling sticks for the coal fires. After lighting the fires in the partner's rooms it was my job to dust their desks, everything was lifted vertically, dusted underneath and replaced exactly as it had been. You have no doubt seen the Black Rod at the opening of Parliament but in Mr Claude's room there was the 'Black Rod of Middleton Cheney', which really was a black rod about four feet long and made of a dark wood like ebony. When I had dusted his desk I used to give this black rod a polish as well.

There was one office above the street door which was kept locked, and no one was allowed to enter because the occupant has 'Gone off to the war and never come back'. As the year was 1949 I naturally assumed that this meant the 1939-45 war, but no, it was the First World War!

By nine the post would arrive and had to be sorted and taken to the people to whom it was addressed. Mr Arthur would allow me to unpack any consignments of books, which meant that I was able to admire the beautiful leather-bound books with the gold lettering and take the packaging away when I left the room. Then followed the daily delivery described above, and by about 10.30 in the morning I was free to do any other jobs required. One of the partners had a daughter who was an excellent pastry cook and occasionally gave him some cakes to take to the office. On those occasions when

he had overeaten at lunch time he was unwilling to hurt her feelings by not eating them that he would ask the office boy to act as his taster, eat the cakes and give him a report on them. This was the office boy's 'perk' (not a word to anyone mind!).

I liked working for Mr Ward. The best way I can think of describing Mr Septimus Ernest Ward was as Banbury's equivalent of Rumpole of the Bailey. His title was 'The Clerk to the Justices' Clerk' and he gave me the impression of knowing everything about everybody in Banbury. He had an old manually operated typewriter, which he hammered unmercifully with a whirr of podgy fingers, but he also had a talent for calligraphy when an old document needed something adding to it. Once he sent me up into the space under the eaves to find a bundle of old papers and bring them to him. He found the document he wanted, which may have been on parchment or vellum which wouldn't go into the typewriter, studied it carefully and told me to mix some black powdered ink to his instructions, then he selected a pen and practiced on a piece of scrap paper for a while (similarly to Mr Lowe) and, when he was able to produce a script like the original, he worked on the document slowly and carefully. A sprinkle of powder and the job was done.

All apprentices and lads are familiar with being sent by the older men to the stores for 'a long stand' or 'striped paint'; I think Stocktons' equivalent was the collection of the 'feof-farm rents'. One day I was given a list in a notebook and told to go and collect them. They were strange peppercorn rents from some of the oldest buildings in the town. There were amounts like 2s 6d from the Whateley Hall Hotel, 1s from the Woolpack, and 10d from the Unicorn in the Market Place. When I returned to the office having collected about 90 per cent of the rents, I was greeted with incredulity: no one had ever succeeded in collecting nearly all the feof-farm rents in one trip.

As I wrote at the beginning, my finishing time in the evening was supposed to be five-thirty, which gave me an hour to cross the Horsefair and the Peoples Park to my home at No. 22 Bath Road, have a quick snack and get to my typing classes at a place between the District Bank and the White Lion by half past six. Unfortunately one of the partners regularly left the office at eleven to start his lunch hour, returned to the office around half-past three or four and then started dictating to his secretary; I was supposed to hang on to take his letters to the post office; many times I didn't get home until half past six which made it a ten-hour day as I had started at half past eight in the morning. I was only fifteen but I saw no reason to let myself be taken for a mug and work a ten-hour day for twelve and a tanner. I stuck the job out from July to the following spring when one day, during my morning round, I saw a small notice in the window of the Midlands Electricity Board: 'Junior Clerk Wanted'. I applied and was set on at over £2 a week, although I had to work Saturday mornings. And so I started my second job.

About fifty years later I had to call in to Aplins of West Bar on business and there on the wall in the hall was the brass plate from outside the front door of Stockton, Sons & Fortescue! Many times I have wondered what course my life would have taken had I remained with them and what became of my Dickensian desk with its encouraging plaque and the Black Rod of Middleton Cheney.

Alan Sargeant
Prize-winning entry

The Record Shop

My first job was at Haydn Heard, a shop selling records and accessories, situated at the High Street end of Banbury's Church Lane. Founded by the late Mr Heard, and later managed by his daughter Barbara, the shop was a family business with three members of staff including myself. This was in November 1975 when singles cost about 40p and LPs £3.99, and at a time when Church Lane was an extremely busy thoroughfare, especially on Saturdays. Half-day closing was on Tuesdays, but Haydn Heard was shut all day, enabling me to have a whole day off during the week.

I started work there on a weekly wage of £13 after a year at North Oxon College where I studied after leaving Chipping Norton Comprehensive School at sixteen. At the time I travelled to and from Banbury by Midland Red bus (usually a double-decker); the single fare cost approximately 37p for the 12-mile journey, which seemed to take forever as the bus lumbered around South Newington and Wiggington on the evening return journey: on my first day at work I slept all the way home. If it started to snow while I was at work I usually had to leave early, as the buses would cease to run at the slightest sign of bad weather.

The shop itself was quite small; the front part contained the counter, singles, pop LPs and cassettes. Classical records were displayed at the rear of the shop, which also housed three booths for customers who wished to listen to a record before deciding whether or not to purchase it. Naturally the local teenagers used to ask for the latest releases to be played for them with no intention of buying, after a while though you became used to the same faces and knew who to say 'no' to. Haydn Heard also

Bridgett Lucas on the then unfinished Ruscote estate, mid-1970s.

soared into the 90s several times. Due to its location, temperatures in the shop only reached the mid-70s, though we still consumed copious supplies of ice cream from Dillon's in Parsons Street. June 1977 brought with it the Queen's Silver Jubilee and the window of Haydn Heard, along with that of almost every other shop, was decked in patriotic colours. As part of the celebrations and to continue the theme I dressed for work in red white and blue, with my fingernails painted to match. That summer also saw Virginia Wade in the Wimbledon singles finals, and we listened to the match in the shop on a radio brought in by my boss.

Between 1977 and 1978 the prevailing fashion in music and clothes was punk,

stocked such items as cases to hold records and cassettes, recorders, ocarinas and kazoos, metronomes and music stands. I remember hoping that any customer buying a music stand would not ask for a demonstration of how to put up the stand as I could never remember how to do it, despite being shown several times.

Christmas 1975 came soon after the job started and with it came the release of Queen's *Bohemian Rhapsody* and its record-breaking sales. At the time it seems as if the only item we were selling was that particular recording. During the heat wave of 1976 Haydn Heard was a respite from the heat outside which

Later, in the garden of her Chipping Norton home.

with bands such as the Sex Pistols storming the charts. When *Never Mind the Bollocks* was released we displayed, after much discussion, a sleeve from the album in the shop window. However, following complaints from the manager of the shop opposite it was soon removed. Punk fashions ensured that we had some colourful customers for a couple of years. The death of Elvis Presley caused a massive run on all his recordings. One particularly amusing incident occurred following the death of Bing Crosby. An album of his was released posthumously, and shortly afterwards a lady came into the shop requesting a copy of this LP, followed by the question, 'Did Bing Crosby record this before or after he died?'

My employment in the shop brought several notable moments and perks such as free tickets to see Cliff Richard in concert at Oxford, given to me by reps from EMI. Also, standing in the shop doorway on a quiet Wednesday afternoon my colleague and I were amazed to see Kenny Everett strolling up Church Lane unrecognized by any of the passers-by. During my employment at Haydn Heard shops such as Boots and W.H. Smith had moved into bigger premises in Banbury and started to stock records and cassettes, selling them at greatly discounted prices. This signalled the beginning of the end for many independent retailers including Haydn Heard and business slowed considerably during the late 1970s. Consequently in the early spring of 1979 Haydn Heard sadly and finally succumbed to the prevailing trading conditions and closed its doors for the last time.

Bridget Lucas

CHAPTER 6

Personal Memories

Some of Banbury's youth enjoying an evening at the Winter Gardens in the 1950s. The Winter Gardens, owned by Mrs Usher, was a place where the young gathered for roller-skating, discos, and all manner of fun, till its closure in the early 1980s. (Supplied by Martin Blinkhorn)

Childhood

My father, Joseph Nunn, was a local lad born in Calthorpe Street in 1919. During the Second World War he was stationed for a while in Coleraine (Northern Ireland), where he met and later married my mother Eileen Wilson on Christmas Day 1941. After the war was over they eventually moved back to Banbury with their young son, my brother Terence. My father was an incredibly patient and gentle man, whose main concern was for his family. My mother too, was gentle and kind, and was also full of fun. As brothers go mine was very good really – although I'm told that when I was little he used to dig pits, cover them with leaves, and then try to make me walk across them (I was never quite that stupid). Though money was in short supply I've always classed myself as very lucky to be born into such a loving family.

By the time I was born my family had moved into a new house in Cherry Road, which is where I spent my formative years. This was a pretty good place to live: you knew all the families around the street, and you usually ended up playing with their children if they were around the same age. At the time there were families, such as the Prescotts, the Lawleys, the Greens, and of course the Joneses! Mrs Jones was my mum's best friend: both being Celts (one Scottish and the other Irish), they got on well together, each being full of fun, with good senses of humour. Aunt Nell soon became a firm favourite with me (and still is), and she would have to try to sneak past the gate – for if I saw her, there would be no peace until she came in.

The thing I remember most about my childhood was the 'fun' we had. As children we spent hours playing such games as 'Queenie Queenie Who's got the Ball', 'Jacks' and 'Please Mr Crocodile'. 'Knock a Door Ginger' was a favourite: one child, usually the smallest (I was never that tall), would creep up to the victim's door and attach cotton to the knocker. This would then be unwound and trailed back to the rest of the gang hiding behind some hedge. The door would then be knocked via the cotton, which would break when the door was opened, leaving the 'victim' confused as to who had knocked. This may have fooled them sometimes, but at other times they must have seen the gang of kids in the street or heard sniggers from behind the hedges. Most people were good-natured about our

Terence Nunn in the garden of his Cherry Road home.

Aunt Nell in the early 1950s with, from left to right, Jimmy, Margaret, Malcom and Eleanor.

Eileen Nunn with her son, Terence, in 1944.

Joseph Nunn holding his daughter Janice, with son Terence in 1955.

game, but you knew when they'd had enough, and would clear off. Some houses were avoided, especially if complaints to your parents were in the offing. One of my favourite games was 'Fox and Hounds': the foxes went off to hide in gateways, gardens or behind hedges, and would be hunted down by the hounds. The boundary that we set for hiding was between the Fairway and Withycombe Drive as this was where the fields started (at the time Hastings Road and the Bretch Hill estate hadn't been built). This was especially thrilling if played in the dark. Home was always the lamp-post outside the Reeds' house; if you managed to reach this without being tagged, then you were safe.

Your parents always knew where you were, they just had to look outside or listen

for your shouts or screams, if a rowdy game was in progress; that is until bedtime! Then mysteriously, when they came out to call you in, there would not be a child in sight. We would all have legged it, trying to snatch a few illicit moments more, and then would plead ignorance of the time when we eventually returned home. Sometimes you got away with it, though mostly not, but it was always worth it!

As a child you always wanted a bike: when I was small I had a three-wheeler, and not surprisingly, it was inevitable that its intended use would be perverted. One child would pedal, another would stand on the back, and the third would sit on the handlebars. As much speed as possible would be obtained and then we would whiz off down Cherry Road. We did not always make the turn at the bottom, sometimes ending up in the hedge or on the verge; however, if you managed to get round on two wheels that was considered a great success. When I was older I had a second-hand two-wheeler: one day, when we had been racing around, I started to pull into the kerb and the next thing I remembered was waking up on the sofa at home. It appears that on hitting the kerb I went flying over the handle bars, knocked myself out, and had to be carried home by a neighbour. I managed to get two weeks off school and some spectacular scratches and cuts on my face out of it. Unfortunately most of these had healed before I returned to the sick fascination of my school friends.

There was only my brother and myself in our family, but my best friend Sue Bryan was from a family of thirteen, so one more child did not make much difference. The older siblings, such as Judy, would always keep an eye on the younger ones and during the summer holidays and at weekends we used to spend as much time as possible playing up the fields. We would make camps out of the straw bales, climb trees, paddle in the brook, or simply explore. One of the older boys had tied a rope with a piece of wood knotted to it from an overhanging branch of a tree at the top of the bank. You could then climb the bank, grasp the wood, and swing yourself up and out over the drop. At the pinnacle of the swing, you would then let go to fall into the pile of straw that had been heaped beneath. One day I spotted my parents out for a walk, I pleaded with the older kids to let me 'have a go' and shouted to my parents to watch. As I was too small to reach the handle I had to be lifted up and pushed out. However I was unable to hold on for long and didn't quite make it to landing on the piled up straw; but it didn't matter, feeling

exhilarated I rushed up the bank to join the end of the queue for my next go, sporting an ear splitting grin.

As well as the games and playing out in the fields, another favourite pastime of Sue and myself was to play tricks on Mum. This generally involved either frightening the life out of her by diving through the window from behind the curtains, whilst she was watching television, or by pouring water down onto her from the upstairs window, whilst she was gardening. Despite these childish pranks I could be known to be constructive in play. One Hallowe'en some one thought it would be a good idea to make pumpkin head lanterns, and as we didn't have any pumpkins we used swede instead. Many hours and sore fingers later we were the proud owners of hideous, ghoulish, lanterns. Unfortunately it was still daylight and as we couldn't wait for darkness, an alternative was needed. I should imagine Mr Bryan was quite startled when on opening the coalhouse door; he was confronted with six hideous glowing faces, supported by six grubby kids.

A visit to the cinema was considered a to be a special treat. They used to show two films, and more often than not the 'B' film was the better of the two. I vividly remember my parents taking me to see *St Trinians* at the Essold in Banbury, and on being led skipping from the cinema, I expressed a desire to attend such a school: my father thought that I would fit in just fine. Saturday morning pictures were a highlight of the week; though if money was scarce, you might have had to hunt around for Corona pop bottles to return to fund the excursion. We would all gather at Julie Cummings's house where she would usually cook a 'fry up' (more than likely without her parents' knowledge), after which (we were

usually running late by this point), we would have to run for the bus that would take us into Banbury. The Grand Cinema was in Broad Street (this is now a Chicago Rock Café), and on a Saturday morning an extremely disorderly queue of noisy, over-excited kids could be found outside its doors. The queue was patrolled by what we referred to as the 'heavy gang'; these were older kids chosen to keep order, and they did so, very heavy-handedly!

In the foyer you could purchase your tickets and sweets. Tickets for downstairs were sixpence, and tickets for the balcony were ninepence. Usually we went downstairs, but if you had managed to get enough money or were willing to walk home, you would go upstairs. Up in the balcony you just had to get on the front row, always remembering to check your seat before sitting down, as it might have been wet, or have something sticky on it. The coat would then have to be screwed up and quickly sat upon before your so-called friends had the chance to throw it over the balcony into the marauding mob below. If this happened you would watch as your one and only coat (the one that you would either grow into or that would last a bit longer) sailed over the balcony, arms akimbo, with the contents of your pockets spewing out across the crowds into the heaving mass of childish savages. On noting approximately where your coat had landed you would then have to ask the usherette if you could go down to retrieve it. She would escort you to recover the trampled rag, which you would then have to wear to church on Sunday and school on Monday, and explain the reason for its sorry state to your mother. The quick retrieval of the coat however was very much dependent on the mood of the usherette. If the little monsters' behaviour had annoyed her that week then you would have to wait for her convenience.

An important survival technique to remember when sitting downstairs at the Saturday morning shows was never to sit directly in front of the balcony. This was because some kids had 'nasty habits' and you were never sure what would land on your head. The air would be full of 'missiles' and the noise level unbelievable, and when the lights went down and the 'Minors of the ABC Club' song was bellowed out (mutilated of course), the programme would begin. The programme consisted of cartoons, a film and of course, an antique serial where the hero performed death defying feats, ending in what must surely be his death – to be continued 'same time, same place, next week': of course the next week you would see him jump out of the crashing car before it plunged over the cliff. Sometimes the lights would go up half way through the programme; this generally spelt trouble. The manager would appear and threaten closure if the noise did not cease. If the film was interesting there was a fair chance the behaviour would improve, but sometimes some could just not control themselves, and if this happened the film would be stopped and we all had to leave, never knowing how the film ended. I remember sitting there, hoping that they would all shut up so that I could see the end of the film. After the show was over we would all charge off to catch our bus, or start the trek home through Peoples Park – usually re-enacting what we had seen.

Janice Nunn

Hill View and Drayton School

My most vivid memory of Hill View School is of my younger brother nearly dying there. The school had a small stream that separated it from the playing field; it was generally used for racing stick boats, collecting shrimps, or chucking other kids in. It ran all the way across the school, and ended in a boggy swamp outside my classroom. The swamp was fantastic: if there was a new kid he would be found weeping as his shoe, or school bag sank in to what we imagined were its depths. We would throw rocks into it, bricks, anything that would make a good noise as it hit. One of my friends once stole a shopping trolley from the local shop and threw that in. It took a long time to sink, but eventually there was nothing left of it to be seen. I only ever saw one thing go in there that came out again: my younger brother. I must have been about nine at the time, and I am sure that Lee, my brother, was three. My mum was picking me up from school, and she had brought Lee with her; I think he was in a pushchair, but cannot be sure. My mum was talking to some other parents as Lee escaped from his chair (if he was in it; if not he just escaped) and made his way over to the swamp. No one saw him getting closer to it, and no one saw or heard him fall in, (although I'm sure that my friends and I would have approved of the noise he made hitting the bog). When we noticed he was missing, a mild panic started, ending in fully-fledged terror. Everyone searched, and shouted for him, but he seemed to be nowhere. Eventually one of the mothers screamed and pointed at the swamp, I clearly remember that she could say no words, just strangled breaths and screams. All that could be seen of Lee was his hand sticking out of the swamp. One of the teachers – I like to think it was Mr Eccles, but it was more likely to have been Mr Massey or Mr Lester – pulled him out. I was only slightly disappointed that he did not make a popping noise as he finally left the swamp. He was black with mud and gunk from head to foot, his one clean hand being all that looked human. When he opened his mouth (to scream) the pink of his gums, and the white of his teeth looked bizarre against the mud and leaves that surrounded them. Once he was safe and cleaned up a bit, we left to go home. The only other time Lee caused such an uproar in the school was when he himself was a pupil, and for some reason asked his teacher if she was a lesbian.

This swamp wasn't the only thing at the school that would be considered unsafe. As with most playing areas in the mid-1970s, all of Hill View's playgrounds were either concrete hoops, or upended logs of wood of varying height on a concrete base. More than one pupil was rushed to casualty with a split head or broken ankle. Things like that just weren't an issue then. There is no question that Hill View wasn't a very well run, and mainly safe school. It's just that

Stuart and Robert Lemon pictured together at Hill View School during the 1970s.

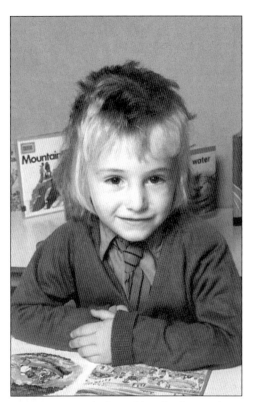

Stuart Lemon looking like 'he'd just been dragged through a hedge backwards' (as the headmaster of Hill View School regularly described him).

attitudes to what is and what isn't acceptable for five- to ten-year-olds to be around has changed.

My other brother, Robert, was also at Hill View whilst I was there; at this age he was incredibly accident prone (he had had over a hundred stitches by his ninth birthday.) One day in the infants he was standing behind a rocking chair when somebody jumped on it, the top of the chair hit his face, causing him to be rushed to hospital for yet more stitches. The doctor stitching Robert's face messed it up, causing him to need plastic surgery at a later date; if you look at our school photos you can see that for a while his lip was out of shape. This was just one of the many hospital visits that my brother had. It wasn't that he was clumsy – it was just that he was always in an incredible rush to do things. He very much acted first, and put up with the consequences later.

My worst memory of the school is the warm milk we were made to drink in the infants. It was usually delivered about an hour before we drank it and I can only assume that it sat in front of a heater until we were ready for it. Every day I used to dread Mrs Woolley giving me my warm half bottle of milk. We were given a straw to drink it through, but by the time we got it the milk was so thick that your ears would bleed before you got any milk from the straw. It had a horrible, thick repugnant taste that I can still taste when I think about it. I was always the last to finish, the other kids just seemed to knock it back and then get on with whatever they were doing. I would sit there for ages, drinking (chewing) a bit at a time, gagging and being almost sick with every mouthful. The teacher would get furious with me and demand I finished it instantly, which made it so much worse. There was nowhere I could tip it away, or hide it so I was forced to drink this foul liquid every day until my parents wrote a letter demanding that I be given orange juice or water instead.

During my time at Hill View, the teachers all seemed to be real characters and more than a little eccentric. The headmaster, Mr Eccles, would always play the piano 'badly' (in the style of Les Dawson) during assembly. He would also pick me out every assembly to show the other pupils what you would look like if you were pulled through a hedge backwards; my hair was huge and odd in those days and Mr Eccles seemed to enjoy laughing at it. He could, however, be a bit of a soft touch; if you were sent to him for the cane and pretended to be scared (a few crocodile tears seemed to help) he would tell you off a bit, but didn't have the heart to cane you. Mr Massey, who would be quiet and sincere one moment, would be shouting and red with anger the next. Miss Price accepted the job at the school after asking God for guidance. She made me stand outside the classroom for laughing at this story, only letting me in about an hour later when she heard me sneezing. Still she was good enough to apologize, and admit that she had forgotten I was out there. I'm sure every Hill View pupil remembers Mr Girling fondly, with his mass of ginger hair and beard. The only really scary teacher was Ms Rowntree. A mixture of Kate Bush and a wailing banshee, she could terrify you with a glance. If she picked up on some bad behaviour of yours, you were doomed.

After leaving Hill View, Drayton School seemed to be a huge and terrifying place. It had a mostly unfair reputation for being violent, and second best to Banbury School, but it taught those willing to listen with care and efficiency. In the first year bullying from older pupils was rife. I was lucky enough to have an older brother, Robert, so mostly I was left alone. Robert held the school record for being on report for longest, a record unlikely to be beaten because it started with his first day, and ended five years later when he left. Most first years were bullied for their dinner money, or for their actual dinner, had they brought in a packed lunch: one unlucky pupil was hung by his feet out of the window on the top floor until he gave up his money, this was a fairly extreme case as most unwilling pupils were just beaten or terrorized.

One of my favourite memories of Drayton School was the day when *Jim'll Fix It* was filmed there. Some girl had written to Jimmy Saville asking for Simon LeBon to be her knight in shining armour. A few months later he turned up in full body armour on a white horse. He knocked on a classroom door, and surprised the girl by taking her away on the back of the horse. She was, of course, thrilled. For the rest of us, it was a fantastic chance to annoy a celebrity. It was a very snowy day, and we came up with the idea of snowballing him as he

Stuart, Robert, and Lee Lemon, pictured with their friend Andrew Paste near their home on the Ruscote Estate.

A class at Hill View School with their teacher, Mr Priest.

left the school. He finished filming his scenes on the white horse, and then came up all of us pupils watching, to say a few hellos and sign some autographs. As he turned his back on us about fifteen pupils let fly with a barrage of snowballs, mostly on target. He turned round, bright red with anger, and swore at us before getting in his limo. The limo then became the target; all the way up the school drive we pelted the limo with snow and ice, watching Simon LeBon screaming at us out of the window. His driver was just trying to see the way out of the school through his now white windscreen. Needless to say, when they showed it on the TV none of this was shown, and although LeBon did not show up at the TV studio I'm sure that was not because

of our treatment of him.

Parents' evening was always dreaded in our house because Robert's teachers always took this opportunity to tell my parents everything that he had done wrong that year. Once, he sat outside while Dad was talking to his teacher. The teacher left after ten minutes and brought back another teacher. Now Robert started to worry, then the door opened again the other teacher left and came back with the headmaster and yet another teacher. Most parents get five to ten minutes per teacher; my dad hat to sit for nearly forty-five minutes with four or five different teachers all telling him where Robert was going wrong. The walk home that night seemed to take forever. Dad didn't say a word all the way home, he just looked at

On his 'Chopper' bike riding down Highfurlong.

Robert in a way that let him know he was in trouble.

The teachers at Drayton in my time were also very memorable. The headmaster, Mr Fairbourn, was very small and thin but was also somehow terrifying. His eyes always seemed to be closed, but he could always see what you were doing. A favourite torture of his was to grab your ear and twist it until you screamed, if you were foolish enough to try not to vocalize your pain he would just keep twisting until you did. One pupil at Drayton through an egg at him as he got in his car, he was never caught which is probably just as well as I hate to think what he would have done to him. My two favourite teachers were Mr Moffat and Mrs Holder. Mr Moffat taught history, with brief lapses into whatever was on his mind that day. He bought history to life, and always considered that teaching should be fun as well as informative. He told me that his pupils didn't realize they were learning until they were asked a question, and were surprised to know the answer. He was never happy with the style of teaching that said you had to copy from a blackboard or book; he would rather entertain and teach at the same time. He was a fantastic teacher because of it. His punishments were always very novel, he would bring a pupil into a class, tell us what he had done wrong and then say 'Right, I have to leave the room for a few minutes. If this lad has any bruises on him when I return, I won't notice them.' Then he would leave, he would always return if it looked like an over-zealous pupil was going to take him up on it, though. Mrs Holder was my English teacher; she was always encouraging and

Stuart Lemon and his friend Steven Trivett.

Sergeant French leading a town council parade. The mace bearer, on this occasion was Norman Dufour.

Edna Sparkes on her wedding day at St Mary's church in 1962.

Edna Sparkes aged nine.

Edna's young family pictured in 1974.

Edna Sparkes's home, Golden Villa, in 1959.

willing to help out. She passed on her love of literature to us and only gave me lines once. There was Mr Kavolic, who was Polish, but taught French. He would give out prizes for the neatest book, and sometimes play bingo with us. He also kept a hammer on his desk and would hit the desk with it as hard as he could if someone misbehaved. Miss Lee was my maths and form teacher. She used to ride with a biker gang and once told me that, as a woman, she had to ride better than all the men or sleep with them all to be allowed into the gang. Mr Salt never seemed to like me very much, and always seemed to enjoy showing me up. The feeling was mutual! Mr Hunter was a very old-fashioned style teacher; he used to enter a rowdy room shouting at the top of his voice, handing out detentions. Most of the pupils and many of the teachers were scared of him. I met him again a few years after I left school; one of my friends answered an ad to buy a car and he was the one selling. He was as surprised as we were, and we ended up talking about other teachers at the school. I wouldn't say that being a pupil at Drayton School was a fantastic experience, but it was definitely an experience that I would have hated to have missed. I drove past Drayton School the other day, just to have a look at the old place, and was saddened to see that most of its playing fields have made way for housing estates. Apart from that it seemed exactly the same as when I was there.

Stuart Lemon

Banbury

'All the old familiar places, that this heart of mine embraces': this line from a 1960s Tony Bennett song evokes for me poignant memories of the disappearing faces of the Banbury that I knew, and that my father knew before me. He was born just up the road in the village of Swerford and later became a 'beat' copper in the Oxfordshire Constabulary, treading the streets of Banbury – his home town.

I too walked the familiar streets of my home town. First as a schoolgirl growing up in Grimsbury, wearing my white cotton ankle socks and Clarks leather sandals (bought from Cluffs on Bridge Street), making my parents proud by passing the entrance exam at Woodgreen Technical School (1953); then as a teenager during the late 1950s in my courting gear – a smart suit from Judges – balancing on 3-inch heels from Railtons. Of course, with no cars, we walked everywhere! Later I rode as a beautiful, optimistic young bride in a Trinder's limo in 1962 and buying my first Timms home for the princely sum of £4,250. Four years later, I'm a pram-pushing mother with my Co-op high-sprung pram, and six years on, pushing a twin pushchair from Trinder's, buying my children's clothes at the Pirates' Den, the Market, and Be Wise, and toys and shoes from the Co-op. Now it seems I've walked full circle – and I'm buying as a grandmother.

Edna Sparkes

CHAPTER 7
Village Life

Sheep at Bowmans Bridge, Clifton.

The Duke of Cumberland's Head, Clifton.

Clifton

It is easy to imagine Clifton as it was sixty years ago. The thatch is long gone, replaced by low-maintenance slate and tile; the growl of diesel-driven four-by-fours has taken over from the clip-clop of horses' hooves; and instead of the clatter of iron cartwheels the muted roar of the motorway floats in the air when the wind blows from the east. But you can still sit quietly in the long grass beside Bowman's Brook and picture the drover passing through with his sheep on his way to Somerton, and the low lying meadows are still transformed into mirrored lakes every autumn, just as they have been for thousands of years.

Clifton is a sleepy hamlet of seventy-five houses and a pub on the eastern boundary of the parish of Deddington. The river

Cherwell marks the parish boundary, as well as the boundary between Oxfordshire and Northamptonshire. The M40 is within sight and sound of Clifton, with the nearest junction about five miles away at Ardley. The nearest main railway stations are Banbury, about 10 miles to the north, or Bicester, 10 miles to the east, with a halt at Kings Sutton, four miles away. The towpath of the Oxford canal, with its brightly painted traditional narrowboats, is a popular walk, just half a mile away across the fields.

A few Cliftonians have lived in the village all their lives but these days most of the people who live there are relative newcomers, attracted to the village by the peace and beauty of the countryside while earning their living elsewhere. The only businesses today are a couple of family farms, an antique shop, a picture framer's, a home for elderly people and a handful of small companies operating from the converted St James's church.

But it wasn't always so. Sixty years ago, before the war, Clifton was a thriving agricultural community with seven working farms, each employing up to three local people as well as supporting their own families. Traditional crops were grown in the fields and most farms also kept a mix of dairy cows, beef cattle, sheep, pigs and chickens. Local smallholders had a few chains of land each and harvested and thrashed their own corn. They kept a few chickens and grew potatoes for themselves and their pig, which would be fattened up in the yard and end up on the table. The miller, George Robinson of Clifton Mill, ground corn for the farmers, which they then used to feed their stock in the winter. Others made their living on the canal, and the railway attracted many workers from the village.

As well as the farms there was a village school (which closed in 1945), a shop, a post office, and Frank Garratt of Home Farm delivered milk straight from the cow to all the houses. Other self-employed tradesmen included Ramsey Sykes, a well-known hedge layer and ditch digger, a wheelwright, and Teddy Mobs, a blacksmith from Aynho who travelled regularly to the forge at Ashley House in Chapel Close to shoe all the village horses – in those days there was only one car. There are still traces of these lower, pastoral times. Peep into the big Dutch barns behind The Chestnuts and you will see two farm carts under their shroud of dust and cobwebs, still proudly bearing the Welford family name.

These days the faithful have to travel to

Clifton Mill during the floods of 1998.

Floods in Clifton, 1998.

Deddington or further afield to worship, but sixty years ago St James's church on the main road was very active and even had its own choir. Consecrated on 10 June 1852, it celebrated its jubilee in June 1903 with a sit-down tea for 146 people! There was also a Methodist chapel in Chapel Close, which was converted into a three-bedroomed home several years ago.

The population and number of homes in Clifton have not changed much in sixty years, although some of the old houses have been replaced with new ones. At the turn of the twentieth century 302 people lived in the village and there were around seventy houses. These days most of the residents own their homes, but before the war most of the agricultural workers lived in tied

cottages, and the railway workers rented theirs. There was much more thatch around in those days too. Clifton Mill House, owned by the Welford family, was thatched, as were many of the farm workers' cottages, which have since been demolished.

These days, as well, the residents of Clifton enjoy the benefits of running water and modern sanitation, although there is still no gas in the village. Sixty years ago ten or twelve houses had their own wells and the rest of the locals had to draw their water from a spring at the mill or from standpipes. Most toilets were outside and emptied after dark by Ramsey Sykes, who smoked a clay pipe while he did it! His odorous task was eventually taken over by the council, who used to send a horse-drawn tanker to collect the sewage. All that's left of those days is the standpipe on the corner of Chapel Close ... and the ghost which, some say, still stalks Pepper Alley, Hartwell Cottage and parts of Walnut Close.

The scenery around Clifton has changed little over the years, although there used to be more willows along the river and Dutch elm disease devastated the native elm population in the 1970s. The low-lying fields to the east still flood the way they always flooded when it rained, and Easter 1998 brought the most spectacular floods in living memory. The road was impassable except by tractor and the ground floor of the mill house was under several inches of water. Retired farmer Donald Welford, whose grandfather owned Clifton Mill, says neither he nor his grandfather ever knew the mill to flood before.

Clifton is rich in native flora and fauna and even the opening of the motorway on 16 January 1991 has made little difference to the numbers of birds and animals to be seen. Foxes, roe and muntjac deer, badgers, hares and rabbits abound; and the bird population attracts 'twitchers' from all over the country. The skies above the meadows fill with the sounds of the skylark during the spring and summer, and, and visiting waders flock in when the wetlands flood in the late autumn and spring. The biggest decline has been in the numbers of otters and water voles and many locals link this to the increase in mink, which have become a pest.

Now, in 2001, Clifton is a charming place to live. The old ways may have passed into history but the rural traditions of friendliness and community spirit will undoubtedly continue into the future.

Jackie Williamson

St Peter and St Clare's church at Fenny Compton.

Mr. A.J. Knightm, Fenny Compton's carrier.
For years Mr Knight would go to and from
Banbury taking and collecting all manner of
items required by the villagers.

Fenny Compton

*The twenty-year period from the mid-1930s
until the mid-1950s brought major changes to
the way life in England. For six of those years,
1939-1945, England was at war and the village
of Fenny Compton, which is situated about
eight miles north of Banbury, was affected in the
same way as other parts of the country.*

Pre-War
During the late 1930s, the parish consisted
of approximately 160 houses with a
population of 450. The majority of the
dwellings were built of local stone with a
tiled or slate roof. There were some twenty
thatched houses and about eight roofed
over the thatch with corrugated iron. Re-
thatching being an expensive business,
owners had found it necessary to cut costs.
Very few houses were owner-occupied.
Over the previous ten years Southam
District Council had built thirty-two
houses of red brick. The water supply came
from springs on the hills overlooking the
village via two large tanks at the halfway
point. A few pumps and wells were still in
existence from earlier times. Until the
very late 1930s many of the houses did not
have water piped directly to them. The
daily needs of householders were carried in
buckets from the communal taps situated
around the parish. Every drop for washing,
drinking and general use had to be carried;
to live near a tap was a luxury of life.

Prior to 1939, the vehicles based in
Fenny Compton numbered eight lorries,
four vans and ten private cars. Travel was
usually by foot, bicycle or train. The trades
and services consisted of the post office,
Co-operative Stores, a butcher's shop, a
saddler's shop and the Red Lion Inn. They
were all based in the High Street. The
doctor's surgery, the school and general
store were dotted around the village. The
two railway stations stood side-by-side
with the Fenny Compton Garage being
close to the George and Dragon at The
Wharf. The Victoria Arms was about a
mile nearer to Banbury at the tunnel.

Mr Arthur Sumner, the coal merchant,
supplied Fenny Compton and surrounding
villages. Milk and newspapers were
delivered to the houses. The presence of a
village policeman maintained law and
order. A permanent 'lengthman' or
roadman kept the roads and grass verges
free of litter and unwanted vegetation, and

a working man's average wage was about £2 per week. Mr A.J. Knight, the founder of the haulage firm still in business, had been the village carrier for over forty years. As his grandson Keith was my best friend I had regular contact with him. Using a horse and cart, he travelled to Banbury every Thursday, and for a charge of twopence he would take or collect any item of food or footwear. The latter would be prior to or after the attention of Mr Batts in Parsons Street. The fishmonger's shop of Mr Truss – almost next door – was another regular port of call.

Agriculture was the principal industry employing the major part of the labour force. The two railway companies required many workers as stationmasters, porters, platelayers and signalmen, and up to fifteen men were on the books of the County Council, working as lengthmen or in a road repair gang. The education department of the County Council was responsible for the staffing of the school where three teachers taught between sixty and eighty children. The two haulage companies required six drivers. There were several self-employed plumbers, builders and joiners; and the doctor and the rector cared for the medical and spiritual needs of the parishioners.

Very few married women were in full-time occupations other than in a family business on farms or in shops. After leaving school and before marriage, girls were often employed in large houses as cooks, cleaners and housemaids, known as being 'in service'. As no National Health Service existed, Dr Hasluck, the general practitioner, did introduce what could have been classed as an insurance scheme for patients. A few pence per week could be paid into a fund to help, should sickness strike any member of the family. Many

Fenny Compton.

95

adults suffered from TB and severe bronchitis. Young people were often taken ill with measles, scarlet fever, diphtheria and whooping cough. The doctor was a very compassionate man. If he realized a patient could genuinely not pay a bill, he would waive it and there the matter ended.

The village school was divided into three rooms: Infants, Juniors and Seniors. The infants, aged between four and six, were taught by Miss Tomkins; Mrs Olive Sheasby was the juniors' teacher, and the head teacher, Mr Fred Moore, kept control of the senior children from the age of eleven until they left school during the first holiday after reaching their fourteenth birthday.

The leading National Hunt jockey at that time was Gerry Wilson. He lived in Fenny Compton when he won the Grand National in 1934 and the Cheltenham Gold Cup in five consecutive years, 1932-1936. All successes were on the same horse, Dolden Miller. Gerry was my schoolboy hero.

Wartime

For many months before war was declared, a certain amount of preparation for such an event was being made publicly. Obviously a far greater effort went on behind the scenes. Conscription of civilians to the armed forces was the major event taking place in 1939. During the time the war lasted, about fifty young men and women were called up from Fenny Compton. Although the initial enlistment age was between twenty-one and twenty-five years old, this was later widened to between eighteen and thirty. I remember a man who, owing to his experiences in the First World War, was very upset over his son's call-up. National Service continued for some years after the peace was

Fenny Compton.

96

Avon Dassett Road, Fenny Compton.

declared. I was one of the last to be called up. Before my official date, I had volunteered and been accepted for RAF service. Becoming impatient, I wrote to the Air Ministry asking whether they had forgotten me. My father saw what I was doing and reprimanded me, 'You wouldn't be doing that if you had to go to Norton Barracks like I did in 1915.' 'Ah,' I replied, 'I'm not going to Norton Barracks.' About a week later, my call-up papers came I was instructed to join the British Army – at Norton Barracks, Worcester. Someone at the War Office must have had a funny sense of humour!

All civilians were issued with ration books. Fair and equal distribution was made which would not have been so had food been available to the highest bidder. Commodities could still be exchanged for high sums of cash on the black market. When items of food were purchased, a coupon from the ration book was handed over. I do have the remains of an old ration book but amounts of any type of food were not defined as they changed from time to time. Before 1939, about 60 per cent of all food consumed in England was imported. When ships were sunk by sea or air attack it is easy understand why rationing had to be introduced, to ensure fair shares for all. Food was still being rationed in 1950. Stores did, on occasions, receive deliveries of 'extras'. 'Extras' were groceries, cigarettes or other items that were not rationed but in short supply. Tinned fruit comes to mind. When this happened, the staff at Fenny Compton Co-op were quick off the mark in putting the items to one side for friends and family. Very little ever found its way to the general public.

More men were drafted into the police force. Known as special constables, they received limited training and their duties

High Street, Fenny Compton. At the bottom is the war memorial, which was erected in memory of the Fenny Compton men who lost their lives during the First and Second World Wars.

were to assist the existing police who were in greater demand. The village force suddenly increased by 100 per cent when Mr Jim Mold teamed up with PC Jack Wright. One of the constables' main tasks was enforcing the blackout law, under which no building was allowed to display any form of light during the hours of darkness. Dwelling houses used wooden shutters or heavy curtains to prevent any light showing from windows. Some sort of baffle had to be put into doorways, usually a porch, to stop any light showing through. I do not remember anyone being prosecuted for breaking the law. Fenny Compton did not have street lighting before the war so there was no problem in that department. All the blackout precautions were taken to prevent enemy aircrews obtaining any idea where there was human presence or activity below. Motor vehicles were fitted with a 'fruit-can'

type of object over the headlights which caused what glimmer of light shone from them to point downwards onto the road.

High on the list of priorities immediately the war began was to evacuate as many children as possible from areas seen as being vulnerable to air attack. In some cases, mothers did accompany them. The Women's Voluntary Service in Fenny Compton made arrangements with residents to receive children from Coventry for an indefinite period. Wherever possible, all children of a family were billeted together, and teachers from the school they attended in Coventry came with them. They received tuition at various times in the school, the Reading Room and the Oddfellows' Hall. In 1945 Miss Bateman, one of the teachers from Coventry, married Mr Moore the village head teacher, who had been a widower for many years. He retired with his new wife to Coventry shortly afterwards.

As more labour was required in agriculture, the Women's Land Army was formed. The girls were all volunteers and mostly eighteen to thirty years old. Many had hardly ever seen a grass field, never mind milked a cow, as the majority of them came from towns and cities. About twelve girls came to Fenny Compton from Birmingham and were billeted in part of the Lodge in 1942; they went out to farms daily to work. On seeing some calves, one girl asked a farmer 'Are they cow-lets?' and he replied 'No, they are bull-lets!' The young men had a field day! Later some came to be boarded at private houses. Many of the girls married local men and continued to live in the countryside.

In the autumn of 1942 as a member of No. 1460 (Banbury) Squadron Air Training Corps, I experienced my first flight from Chipping Warden airfield with Sq/Ldr Fadden, three crew members, and two other cadets, making our way to and over Fenny Compton on a Sunday afternoon in a Wellington bomber. We made three circuits of the village at a height of 2,000 or 3,000 feet. Circling Fenny Compton for the third time the pilot asked us if we'd like to get out to save cycling home. A lasting memory! When the 'Wings for Victory' week was planned nationally to raise money to purchase aircraft, no organization came forward to arrange a fund-raising dance in the village. The rector asked if the boys of the ATC and the girls of the GTC could get together one evening. The head teacher, gazing over his glasses, replied, 'By what I hear, they get together most evenings!'

Red Lion pub, Fenny Compton.

After the war, in 1947, the names of the six servicemen who gave their lives for their country in the Second World War were added to the twelve names remembered from the First World War on the village war memorial.

Post-war

The 1950s arrived. Change in the home had begun and would continue, electricity being the basis of that improvement. No longer would the chore of washing clothes be carried out in an outhouse or shed half-way down the garden. The washing machine brought a much easier, less laborious way, all within the house. Refrigerators and freezers meant food could be stored or parts used and kept for a later date. The old black kitchen range was replaced with an open fire. The cooking that had taken place in the oven at the side of the fire could now be done with the aid of electricity. A decent sewerage system, I believe, was the greatest improvement ever to take place. Televisions also found their way into many homes, mainly 9-inch sets. Neighbours went to each other's houses to view the television, and it was often difficult to get them out; another miracle had taken place!

As the 1950s arrived so did the motor car. To this time the number had remained constant, with ten or so in the village. Young men many not long demobbed from the forces jumped into the car market. Many cars on offer were 1930s models that had been the prized possession of a professional or businessman over the previous fifteen or twenty years. Having served their purpose with one owner they were about to start a new life with another. The majority of the vehicles were Austin 7s, Morris Oxfords or Ford 8s, my first choice, and changed hands for about £130. We looked on the cars as luxury travel. There was no self-starter (they were started by a handle), no fuel gauge, no heaters or demisters and windscreen wipers were operated by hand.

John Unnitt

CHAPTER 8
Notable Figures and Warkworth Castle

The Hortons are buried in a family tomb at Middleton Cheney. Pictured here is William Horton.

From Parish Fugitive to Lord of the Manor

Anybody in the Banbury area who needs medical treatment that requires hospitalization is admitted to the Horton, but why 'Horton'? Why not Banbury, North Oxfordshire or Cherwell? The answer lies in the name of a man who was an outstanding entrepreneur and industrialist of his time.

William Horton was baptized at St Mary de Castro parish church in Leicester on 19 April 1744. His father, Joseph Horton, gave his occupation in the parish register as maltster (i.e. brewer); his mother was not named. However, a will written in February 1769, just three weeks before Joseph died, refers to his wife Mary; four sons – William, Joseph, John and Charles, and a daughter, Sarah. William's father appears to have been a relatively prosperous citizen. Records show him to have been a Freeman of the Borough of Leicester, renting land in the parish and disputing the rent he was expected to pay! William may have worked with his father for a number of years, as he did not start a seven-year apprenticeship with his uncle, John Horton, a blacksmith, until 1765 when he had reached the age of twenty-one. This was relatively late, as most apprentices would have started at fourteen. In 1771 the apprenticeship was transferred to Isaac Colnet and William was released from the Blacksmiths' Company in February 1772.

As a young and possibly irresponsible man, William was obliged to abandon an unknown young lady of his acquaintance who found herself in an unfortunate predicament. He hurriedly left his home town, 'through an error common to young men who, sooner than enter a state of matrimony, chose to fly from the parish officers.' At that time the father of an illegitimate child could either have been sent to prison by the magistrate or made to pay a sum of money until the child was of an age to be apprenticed or put to work. Of course, the other alternative was marriage but William does not appear to have regarded this as an option.

We do not know why he settled in Chacombe, although the availability of work was no doubt a deciding factor. The growth of the hosiery industry in this area had been accelerated by the Enclosure Acts of the 1760s when many unemployed agricultural labourers turned to the knitting of hose for employment. William commenced employment in the village as a stocking-frame repairer and setter-up; it is certain that he developed an intimate knowledge of the principle and working of the machines. An enterprising young man, he was driven by a consuming passion to modify and enhance the process of making silk stockings. William was convinced that he could improve and speed up the production and his ultimate aim was to produce an elastic and sound fabric.

Working a stocking frame required considerable physical effort, both from the operator's hands and arms, which moved the carriage, and from the feet and legs, which moved the treadles. Good sight was also needed as the machine required frequent adjustment. A flat piece of material was produced, which could be widened or narrowed to follow the shape of the leg. The basic shape was then seamed up to form a fully-fashioned stocking. Women usually undertook the seaming, whereas the strenuous exertion required to operate the frame was usually the man's job. Children or women wound the thread from hanks or bobbins. Framework knitting, as it came to be called, was therefore a cottage industry in which all the family participated and one that could be carried out at home since only muscle power was needed.

William's finances were low while he worked in his spare time to construct a new frame, capable of producing the improved stockings that he felt would make his fortune. Financial disaster threatened when he was delivering a new, ordinary stocking frame to a client by packhorse. The frame was insecurely tied to the animal's back and was severely damaged when it fell off, resulting in the loss of its value, an estimated £20 (equivalent to perhaps £800 today). William was in total despair and considered another clandestine removal to escape the claims of his creditors. However, a friend assisted him with the money and in the spring of 1772 he went to live at the great seat of fashion, London, where he succeed in finishing his modified frame.

The firm expanded in subsequent years and in 1790 the partners set up further establishments at Nottingham and Godalming in Surrey. William increased the size of two of his frames which greatly excited the Surrey workmen who named them Gog and Magog. However, they refused to work a cloth on them greater than 36 inches wide, until a giant of a man called James Whitehorn stepped forward to take up the challenge. He worked Magog for over twenty years; making fleecy greatcoats upon it and driving it faster than ordinary hands could work the normal size frames. The frames at Godalming specialized in fleecy underclothing, particularly for use by sufferers of gout and rheumatism. It is not known if William Horton had a personal interest in these items! Other products included muff linings, bootikins and coach carpeting. It is recorded that 'most excellent and durable articles were made' and that the partners supplied 'the Nobility and Gentry' with outstanding quality goods. Evidently by 1797 the demand was so great that 'a thousand silk knotted frames could furnish but a scanty supply'.

The registering of patents did not always prevent illegal copying and on one occasion an agent from another firm in Nottingham pirated William's latest invention and fled to Scotland. William sent his brother to investigate the rival manufacturer with disastrous results for the family. His brother is reported to have died from the consequences of a severe cold caught on his journey north and back.

On 12 August 1777 William married Elizabeth Sufflee, the only child and heiress of Peter Sufflee, a merchant of Hoxton Square in Middlesex. The wedding took place at St Leonard's church, Shoreditch. Appropriately, in William's case, the bells are commemorated in the rhyme *Oranges and Lemons*: 'When I grow rich, say the bells of Shoreditch.'

By 1793 William had progressed professionally to become Master-Warden of the Blacksmiths' Company of London and six years later he had amassed a vast fortune and purchased the Chetwode estate at Warkworth and Grimsbury near Banbury, no doubt choosing this area as his progress to great wealth had started here. He also had a town house in Highbury, then on the outskirts of London. This was a very desirable area where new and elegant houses were built for wealthy residents in the eighteenth century. A further seaside residence at Cliftonville in Brighton and an estate at Brentwood in Essex were additional family assets.

In 1807 William Horton & Son were established as manufacturers of British lace and silk hosiery in Russia Court, Milk Street (not far from St Paul's Cathedral). The location of the business is important as it was conveniently situated near to the Bell and Crown Inn at Holborn. This was the Banbury-London stagecoach link; the journey could be completed in one day for a fare of 16s – half price to passengers willing to travel outside! William was noted as a man of untiring industry and, although he had realized a handsome fortune, at an advanced age he was still to be seen repairing and improving his frames with all the meticulous attention of his younger days. He is reported to have been remarkable for his simplicity of tastes and habits and venerable for his years. He lived to see the coming of the age of machinery to his particular industry with the initial accompanying improvements to pay and working conditions for handloom weavers in this trade. An early census of Middleton Cheney highlights the importance of the textile trade in this area with the following occupations among those listed: ten framework knitters, twenty plush weavers, six weavers, a wool-stapler (i.e. a person that grades wool) and a wool-carder. In his book *The History of Banbury* Alfred Beesley recalls: 'At Middleton and Chacombe there is a considerable manufacture of the finest kind of silk stockings. William Horton Esq., the inventor of the elastic knotted hose, resided in his younger years at Chacombe, and worked there as a Framesmith.'

The death of William Horton in 1833 and the subsequent ending of his business, together with the demise of the cottage industry, severely affected the livelihood of those connected with silk weaving in Middleton Cheney. This is clearly illustrated in a (slightly reworded) extract from a letter written to a relative who had emigrated to Sydney, Australia. 'Middleton Cheney, June 8th 1834. I have had many trials since you left. Myself, it is two years last Whitsuntide since I had any regular work. I have got five children now and the rascally parish would not allow me more then 8s per week for my work; therefore you will easily know my situation ... William Horton Jnr died and the old gent was laid by. His grandson took the business but when we lost William Horton we lost all in a short time after the old boy died. They [Horton and his wife] were both interred at the same time in their family vault. Dear Uncle, you may consider (as you no doubt do) yourself one of the luckiest men in the world, that you have got away from this most trying part of the globe. I pray that God may be with you and yours wherever you be or wherever you go.'

The demise of the silk stocking industry in Middleton was also recalled by George Herbert (1814-1902) in his book *The Shoemaker's Window*: 'The silk-stocking making used to be largely carried on in Middleton Cheney by the Hortons. Since I can remember there was a loom in most of the cottages for the purpose, and now there is not one.'

William Horton and his wife Elizabeth died within two days of each other; they had been married for fifty-six years. Their long and happy life together was a remarkable achievement in an era when one in five marriages would not have lasted ten years, due to the death of a partner. Four sons and daughters had died some years before their parents and the last two sons, William Jnr and Henry George, passed away in 1831 and 1846 respectively. None of the sons married. The family was buried in a family tomb at the Chapel of Ease at Holloway in London. William Horton's fortune eventually passed to his last remaining daughter, Mary Ann, a

Mary Ann Horton, daughter of William Horton, who bequeathed £10,000 in her will to build Banbury's Horton Hospital.

spinster, who also inherited the title and became Lady of the Manor of Middleton Cheney. She built herself a large Manor House known as The Holt in the village, which was demolished some years ago, although the much-altered gatehouse and coach-house remain.

Mary Ann was known for her good works for the poor of the village, especially the children. School records note the gift of clothing for less fortunate children on a number of occasions. She was also responsible for the almshouses being built in 1863 – originally for the workers on her estate. Mary Ann generously contributed to the extensive repairs and restorations to the parish church in 1865, which were carried out under the supervision of George Gilbert Scott Esq., RA, the Victorian architect

whose works included the Albert Memorial in London.

It would appear that in spite of all her charitable works within the area Mary Ann was a lonely lady who mourned the loss of her parents, brothers and sisters. As the last surviving member of the family who had done so much for the people of Middleton Cheney she took the unusual step of erecting a Gothic tomb in All Saints' churchyard, and in November 1865 she arranged for the bodies of her family to be disinterred and brought to the village where their coffins were placed in the new vault. As the building of the Horton tomb coincided with the work on the church there is a distinct possibility that George Gilbert Scott was consulted on its design. The Revd William Buckley conducted the

John Henry Kolle, Mary Ann's nephew.

burial and a large number of village people were present. In fact the schoolmistress, Miss Mary Ayres, recorded that many children were absent on the afternoon of 17 November 'to witness the interment'.

Ironically, Mary Ann, having moved the bodies of her family nearer to her country residence, died herself four years later aged seventy-nine at her house in Highbury, London. Her body was brought to Middleton and she was buried with her family eight days later. The *Banbury Advertiser* printed the suitably moral, Victorian entry on Thursday 22 July 1869: 'Few there are who have left behind them such noble and enduring monuments of benevolence of heart as she whose loss we this day deplore. Go to the village [Middleton Cheney] and there evidence

may be seen on every hand of her wish to promote the comforts of the poor. But in her death the living have a lesson: "Go ye, and do likewise".'

She bequeathed money for the erection of a hospital in Banbury and after her death her nephew and heir, John Henry Kolle, carried out her wishes and allocated £10,000 for the project. The infirmary was originally intended for the poor of Banbury and those living within a ten-mile radius. It was built by Franklin's of Deddington and opened on 17 July 1872, with the provision that there would always be one bed available for a resident of Middleton Cheney. (Mary Ann Horton's will totalled £70,000 – the equivalent of nearly £3 million today).

In the 1990s the Horton tomb had sadly deteriorated and a fundraising appeal was successfully carried out in the village to renovate the memorial. The cost of the restoration was £10,000, the amount it had taken to build the original Horton Infirmary in Banbury.

Sources

Framework Knitting by Marilyn Palmer (1984).
History of Banbury by Alfred Beesley (1841).
History of the Framework Knitters by Gravenor Henson (1831).
History of Machine Wrought Hosiery and Lace Manufacturers by William Felkins (1867).
Shoemaker's Window by George Herbert (1948).
Victorian Banbury by Barrie Trinder (1982).

Acknowledgements

Thank you to everyone who has assisted with my research including Banbury Local Studies Library, Colchester Library, Leicester and Northamptonshire Records Offices, Ruddington Framework Knitters Museum, Godalming Museum, Guildhall Library in London, and the Victoria and Albert Museum.

Nancy Long

Rhubarb and Roses

A glimpse into the life of John Tustain, herbalist and druggist in Milcombe.

Introduction

'The apple trees in full bloom. All Praise to God that I am spared to see such a glorious sight.' These words, quoted from John Tustain's diary for 10 May 1870, show a man very much in tune with God and the beauty of his creation, never to be taken for granted. Until his death in 1873, John lived and worked in Milcombe as a farmer, herbalist and druggist. He grew many plants, some of which today we might call unusual but from which he prepared herbal remedies. Some plants and trees were cultivated for the wholesale market and, together with this enterprise, he grew the conventional farm crops of the period.

Looking at his life from a small number of documented sources, along with one or two family stories, a picture emerges of a hard-working, sensitive and God-fearing man, dedicated to the well being of his family, while seeing to the health of others. He held some official roles in Milcombe. He was churchwarden during the 1840s, and many of the account books dealing with village affairs are in his hand. John as the Enumerator took the census return of 1861. His ability to both write and also keep accounts at a time when few people in Milcombe were literate must have indeed assisted the smooth running of village life.

Early Days

John was born in 1798 and baptized in Milcombe. His mother was Mary, daughter of John and Mary Tustain. They lived in Rose Cottage, and John was a basket maker. It is not known who John's father was; suffice it to say that there are family rumours concerning his identity but no firm candidate has come to light. Mary his mother may well have left the village shortly after his baptism, perhaps in disgrace. She was pregnant again about three years later and a daughter, Sarah, was born in 1802. In 1803 Mary married William Boddington and Sarah was baptized in 1804 as Sarah Boddington. However, it is thought that she was John's full sister and he

John Tustain, herbalist and druggist at Milcombe.

refs to her as such in his will. William and Mary had three children of their own and moved to live at Finstock and Fawler near Charlbury. Mary in later years was a glover and William was probably an agricultural labourer.

John's birth at the onset of the nineteenth century in those circumstances might have placed him at a distinct disadvantage, but surprisingly this does not seem to be the case. During his early youth he acquired some education and was both literate and numerate. This is demonstrated by both his diary entries and the village records.

Family stories state that John's education had been directed and paid for by his father or his family, and that he was supposed to have been sent to train as a doctor in London. There are two theories about why he did not do this. Firstly it was suggested that he failed his exams, and secondly that the financial support required was withdrawn. The outcome was the same for both theories; John returned to Milcombe, where it seems he secured some knowledge of pharmaceutics.

Whilst his early years are something of a mystery, his life does begin to take shape after his marriage in 1828 at Bloxham. John and his wife Elizabeth had eight children who all married and settled locally. There are many descendants. In the 1841 census, John is described as a 'gardener'; he was cultivating the plants which in later years would become the heart of his business. His medical knowledge, albeit limited, began to be useful in Milcombe. Doctors had to be

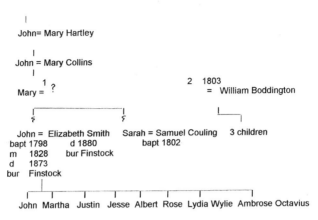

John Tustian's family.

```
             |
        John = Mary Hartley

             |
        John = Mary Collins
             |
          1  ?                              2  1803
       Mary =                                  = William Boddington
```

John = Elizabeth Smith   Sarah = Samuel Couling   3 children
bapt 1798   d 1880   bapt 1802
m   1828   bur Finstock
d   1873
bur Finstock

John Martha Justin Jesse Albert Rose Lydia Wylie Ambrose Octavius

Obituaries from local newspapers :

<u>Banbury Advertiser</u> Jan 16th 1873.

Milcombe

Sudden death - On Saturday last Dr. Tustian for many years practising in this village died very suddenly. Not feeling very well he had gone to bed and was supplied with tea between eleven and twelve. He was left for a short time and on his attendant returning soon after he found him dead. An Inquest was held on Saturday before Mr C.D. Faulkner and a verdict of 'Died from a disease of the heart' was returned. Deceased was 74 years of age and was much respected.

<u>Oxford Times</u> Jan 18th 1873

Milcombe

On Saturday last an Inquest was held before Mr Faulkner Coroner at Milcombe, on the body of Mr John Tustian farmer aged 74. The deceased it appeared had been ailing for some days previous to his death which took place almost suddenly just before eleven O'clock on the morning of the Inquest. He had not been attended by a medical man for upwards of 30 years but when he became so ill a messenger was dispatched for Mr Hyde of Bloxham who was soon after in attendance, but life was then extinct. It was his opinion that a diseased heart was the cause of such a premature death. A verdict accordingly was returned by the jury of which Mr John W. Page was a foreman.

John Tustian died 11th January 1873.

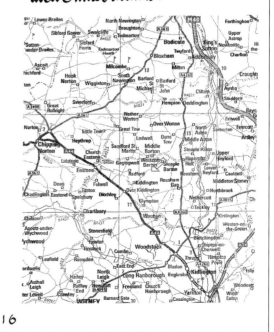

A map showing Milcombe Bodicote and Finstock about twelve miles distant.

16

The Tustain family tree, and obituaries that appeared in local newspapers following John's death.

Telegrams : USHER, BODICOTE.

RICHARD USHER,

Grower and Preparer of Medicinal Herbs, Roots, Rhubarb, etc.,

BODICOTE, BANBURY.

ESTABLISHED OVER A CENTURY.　　　　　　**PRIZE MEDALS.**

Dear Sirs,

　　I beg to submit prices for　　　　　　　　of the undermentioned
Crude Drugs. Samples will be sent free on application. Terms Nett. Free on Rail.

Fol. Belladonnæ, Ang.-Nov., Selected leaves			...	...	...	per lb.
,, ,, ,, Young branches			...	...	...	,,
,, Hyoscyamus, 2nd Bien, Nov., BP 1914			...	...	...	,,
,, ,, ,, ,, BP 1898			...	...	...	,,
,, ,, 1st Bien, Nov.	...	...	...	...	...	,,
Cap. Papaveris, Alb., Ang., Large Size		...	...	...	...	per 1000
,, ,, ,, ,, Medium Size	...	...	...	...	,,
,, ,, ,, ,, Small Size	...	...	...	...	,,
,, ,, ,, ,, Crushed	...	...	...	...	per cwt.
,, ,, ,, ,, Seeds	...	...	...	...	,,
Radix Rhei, Ang., Fine Bold Flat, trimmed		...	...	...	per lb.
,, ,, ,, Small Flat	,,	...	...	...	...	,,
,, ,, ,, Fine Bold Rounds, trimmed (Crowns)		...	,,
,, ,, ,, Small Round Fibre	,,		...	...	,,
,, ,, ,, Decorticated	,,	(Sliced Rounds)	,,
,, ,, ,, Cuttings for Grinding	...	..	...	...	per cwt.
,, ,, ,, Chippings for Grinding	...	...	...	...	,,
,, ,, ,, Pulverised, Finest Quality	...	...	...	per lb.
,, ,, ,, Veterinary Quality	...	...	,,
,, Taraxaci, Ang., Finest Quality, Dried ...	...	...	...	,,
,, Valerianæ ,, ,, ,, ,,	...	...	...	,,

Quotations sent on request for Fresh Herbs, Belladonna, Henbane, Elder Flowers.
Elder Leaves, Red Poppy Petals, Chamomiles, etc., for delivery in season.

ALL OFFERS FIRM FOR MONTH STATED ON THIS LIST.

Richard Usher's Plant List.

called from outside the village when necessary and had to be paid. Villagers could ill afford these visits and treatments, so this is perhaps why John did so well. His so-called 'alternative' medicines were sought enthusiastically and must have had some degree of success as he was even called 'Dr Tustain' in Milcombe and Bloxham.

The Link with Finstock

It is said that at one time John had a disagreement with the vicar at Milcombe and decided to drive to Finstock where his mother lived to attend Sunday services. After each service villagers would 'line the church path' to seek his medical advice. His presence at the following Sunday was eagerly awaited when he would return with the ordered remedies. This connection to Finstock went deeper, for although John did not like to talk about his youth, he must have felt very close to his mother especially when left a widow from 1844. John and his wife were laid to rest in a tomb at Finstock, but there are no memorials to William and Mary. At her passing, Mary was described as a 'pauper' and yet her son ended his days as a successful druggist and herbalist well respected in Milcombe.

Even in his early seventies John's life was very full. He regularly attended to his shop where he sold his remedies and other preparations. He could often be seen tending the crops in season – digging, hoeing, planting and sowing. Preparing medicines such as pills, ointments, tinctures and syrups must all have taken time. John also made frequent visits to the church and chapel in Milcombe – sometimes twice a day. In one entry in his diary he visits the chapel at Bloxham to hear his son Jesse preach and in another he visits the Quakers at the Meeting House in South Newington.

At the same time he was busy keeping accounts, writing letters, sending out sample plant material and supplying various wholesalers in London, Coventry and Birmingham. Chests of herbs etc. would be dispatched by post.

June 1870

Some of the chief plants under cultivation for medicinal and culinary purposes according to his diary were henbane, poppies, lavender, roses and turkey rhubarb, along with hawthorn, larch, ash, oak and various fruit trees. Apple was popular as he made quantities of cider. It is likely that he grew many other herbs such as those on the Ushers' price list from Bodicote. John had a working relationship with the Usher family, described later. Lavender planted with henbane was a popular choice for sweet-smelling products like Lavender water, probably sold in his shop. His daughter Lydia is mentioned in his diary as 'gathering lavender' and 'rubbing and sifting lavender'. Henbane, a biennial extremely poisonous plant, was used externally for analgesic remedies to relieve rheumatism and arthritis. If anyone suffered from toothache in Milcombe, John would have prepared this plant to give relief. It was also an excellent sedative and the whole plant could be used either as powder, tincture, fluid-extract, syrup, infusion or ointment.

John's skills in alleviating pain were often derived from a combination of substances. Extracts from plants such as henbane, hellebore, datura, hemlock and belladonna were very powerful and quite deadly if taken in overdose. A common substance John prepared was opium, derived from the poppy flower. Opium was taken as laudanum or tincture of opium, a combination of opium and alcohol. This is how the drug is described in 1860: 'It is narcotic, sedative and being made with spirit is also to a certain extent stimulant and antispasmodic. For relieving pain wherever situated, to diminish irritation and to procure sleep, it is the best of the medicines we possess.'

The forms of use were powder, syrup, tincture, extract and decoction (the extraction of the water-soluble substances of a drug or medicinal plants by boiling). This also includes the resulting essence or liquor. Much of John's reputation was based on his cultivation and preparations made to sell wholesale. Ladies were supposed to have arrived at his shop to purchase his rose water. Much attention was given to drying the petals, weighing and mixing. Roses and their leaves were used in all kinds of ways medicinally, cosmetically, and for culinary purposes. Conserve of roses prepared with fresh red petals pound in a mortar with three times their weight in sugar and enough quantity of infusion of roses to make consistency like honey, could be taken in quantities of 50-100g per day to aid tubercular and pulmonary complaints.

John packed chests of rose leaves, which were sent to London and cities all over the country. A decoction of leaves – perhaps 30-40g to a litre of water – was boiled for two or three minutes, left to infuse for ten minutes and then drunk at the rate of two or three cupfuls a day to help diarrhoea and dysentery. John would send out samples of rose leaves and a few days later after packing the chests orders would be dispatched.

Just outside Bloxham, between the Barford aerodrome and the carpet factory, lies a small field of just under six acres. This is where John cultivated his roses and other herbs. During June and July when the roses were flowering, the scent and sight must have been amazing. John mentions the labour-intensive hoeing and digging between the rose trees, not forgetting the gathering for which he employed boys and girls. He also talks about the drying of the roses, where they used sheets in the drying room to lay the petals on.

Dried rose petals were used at a concentration of around 40-50g per litre of boiling water to make a lotion to alleviate conjunctivitis and inflammation of the eye, ophthalmia. Women believed that the petals of the apothecary's rose would eliminate wrinkles if rubbed on the skin. Late in the nineteenth century it was proven that roses contained essential oils, potassium and iron.

A more unusual crop John cultivated for medicinal use was turkey rhubarb. It was grown principally for its root and differs from the garden variety we enjoy in pies. Originating from China, it was introduced into England as long ago as 1629. It is a massive plant, the stem reaching anything up to ten feet high. Even a small plantation would look really impressive. All efforts were concentrated on the value of its thick oval-shaped root that had to remain in the ground for three to four years – the longer the better. John sent large quantities all over the country. His original stock was obtained from the Ushers at Bodicote who in turn had purchased it from Dr William Hayward, an apothecary. Dr Hayward had cultivated turkey rhubarb at Bodicote in the late eighteenth century and had received several awards from the Society of Arts in recognition of his efforts. Even at the time of John Tustain's birth in 1798, rhubarb as a useful medicine was gaining the confidence of many doctors in London hospitals. When prepared as a medicine, the drug performed a dual action. The correct dose was vital. It acted as a laxative in cases of constipation and as an astringent in cases of diarrhoea. It could be taken either crushed in infusion or powdered in amounts according to the effect desired.

The roots were dried in John's drying sheds, which may have been located in what is left of his property in Milcombe. The rhubarb was placed on slatted shelves suspended by means of string over heat (around 50 degrees Celsius) from ovens or fires underneath. The first stage of drying placed roots at the highest elevation gradually becoming lower as the process matured. There would be intervening shelves with roots at other stages of the drying process some cuttings were pierced and strung up with string individually and allowed to dry.

While John began his working life as a gardener and probably experimented himself with this plant, only a very small acreage was cultivated, the majority being at Bodicote. In 1845 there was just under ten acres growing in Oxfordshire. There was a steady increase throughout the next fifty years so that by the late 1890s upwards of forty-five acres were supplying turkey rhubarb for medicinal use. In 1847 John was growing around three acres at Milcombe and the rest was grown by Mr Rufus Usher at Bodicote and Overthorpe and by a Mr Edward Hughes at Neithrop in Banbury.

All John's efforts did not go unnoticed for it must have been a great honour to have been chosen to exhibit his prepared plant material at the Great Exhibition of 1851. This exhibit would have been the culmination of expertise and hard work over the years. John collaborated with Mr Usher at Bodicote for part of the exhibit. Cuttings presently preserved in Oxfordshire's museum collections probably resemble those exhibited. They came from Bodicote but whether they are the actual cuttings from 1851 is difficult to say. The writing on the container is remarkably similar to John's. When the cuttings were taken out of their wrapping, a powerful rhubarb aroma arose; this would have been wonderful even if they dated from the early twentieth century. I can only speculate on how John came to exhibit at the Crystal Palace, although locally, committees were set up to choose suitable products for display. John's connection with the Ushers may well have enhanced his position along with his reputation for rose cultivation. I wonder what he thought of the Exhibition – sadly no diary for that period exists. From the pictures and articles about it, the Crystal Palace and its contents must have been an overwhelming sight.

In a codicil to his will in 1872, John shows a compassionate side to his nature. He states that his son John owes him a 'considerable sum of money which it may be inconvenient for him to pay at the time of his decease...' John directs his executors to 'cross and erase the same out of my book and forgive him the debt'. This son had recently been widowed and had eight children. John also includes in his codicil 'any poor person who may owe me any less sum than forty shillings shall not be troubled by my executors to pay the same but they may pay or not as they may feel disposed'.

At the close of his life his wish to be buried at Finstock appears to be John's way of uniting the sadness or disappointment of his youth with his working life in Milcombe, and at the same time binding the Tustain family together.

Jill Adams

The Fall of the House of Warkworth

The years between 1805 and 1815 were a turbulent time. Those dates span the final decade of the struggle against the might of Napoleon, which raged from the battle of Trafalgar in 1805, to that of Waterloo ten years later. Yet, as Jane Austen's novels written during these years show, village life seemed to continue from plough-time to harvest as though hardly touched by the war, and local gossip often concerned people more than foreign correspondence. Those same ten years at the opening of the nineteenth century were to prove very eventful in Warkworth, and were to change the lives of the villagers forever.

It is easy to drive through Warkworth today and not realize you have been there; not even a village sign marks its boundaries, and yet the parish once encompassed Grimsbury, Nethercote and Overthorpe. The church is not easy to spot, because it is not on the roadside, but stands in the midst of farmland, accessible only by a network of footpaths. The castle, however, you will be forgiven for not noticing, because it has disappeared without leaving any trace that it was ever there.

Warkworth Castle was built by Sir Richard Chetwode in 1595, replacing a former manor house that had been erected by his ancestors. It stood just south-east of the parish church on slightly raised ground, and was built of soft, local, honey-brown marlstone, smoothly cut. The elegant façade incorporated classical columns and a great deal of glass, and rose to three storeys. The ground plan formed three sides of a square surrounding a courtyard. As befits the home of an Elizabethan knight and Justice of Banbury, the interior boasted carved oak panelling and a long gallery decorated with heraldic stained glass. The castle estates amounted to 1,073 acres at their greatest extent, consisting of parkland, plantation and fishponds, as well as four tenant farms and several tenant cottages.

Warkworth was sold to the Holman family in 1629. Devout Roman Catholics, the Holmans were cousins of the Viscounts Stafford, and the castle saw action as a Royalist garrison during the English Civil War, but that is not how it came to be destroyed. On the contrary, Philip Holman, sensible chap that he seems to have been, did not play a large part in the war and came through it with his house and estate intact. The Oxford historian Anthony à Wood visited the house towards the end of the seventeenth century, and in his memoirs he explains that he and his kinsman, John Lewes rambled 'To the antient and noble seat of Werkworth, then lately belonging to the Chetwodes; of whom it had then been bought by Philip Holman, of London, scrivener, who, dying in 1669, aged 76, was buried in the church there. ... wee found the eldest son and heir of the said Philip Holman, named George Holman, who was lately returned from his travels, had changed his religion for that of Rome, and seemed then to be a melancholy and bigotted convert. He was civil to us and caused the church dore to be opened, where wee found several antient monuments ... The mannour house is a stately house ... part of which, viz. the former part, was built by the Chetwoods, the rest by Philip Holman, before mention'd.' George Holman's brother, John, was created a Baronet and stood as MP for Banbury in 1661, 1679 and 1681.

Another visitor to the castle was

Horace Walpole, who wrote to his friend John Chute in 1753: 'I forgot to tell you of a sweet house which Mr Montagu carried me to see, belonging to a Mr Holman, a Catholic, called Warkworth. The situation is pretty, the front charming, composed of two round and two square towers. The court within is incompleat on one side, but above stairs is a vast gallery with four bow windows and twelve other large ones, all filled with the arms of the old peers of England, with all their quarterings entire.' No, it was neither fire, sword, nor tempest that finished off Warkworth Castle; it was business, the real-estate business in fact.

The last heiress of the Holmans married Thomas Eyre of Hassop in Derbyshire, and their son Francis Eyre inherited the estate. Through his wife, Lady Mary Radcliffe, he adopted the title Earl of Newburgh, and settled down at Warkworth to a life as one of the leaders of Roman Catholicism in the Banbury area. He was the supporter and patron of several local priests and was quite a pamphleteer in his own right. One of his essays is charmingly entitled: *A Short essay on the Christian religion, descriptive of the advantages which have accrued to society by the establishment of it, as contrasted with the manners and customs of mankind before that happy period. To Which are added, a few occasional remarks on philosophers in general, as also on some of the objections started against the Christian religion by the fashionable writers of the present age. The Whole proposed as a preservative against the pernicious doctrines which have overwhelmed France with misery and desolation. By a sincere friend of mankind. 1795.*

This brings us back to the Napoleonic Wars and almost to the decade that witnessed the end of the Lords of Warkworth. Francis, Earl of Newburgh, died in 1804 and was succeeded by his son, another Francis. The family had numerous estates in Derbyshire, Leicestershire and Hampshire, and the new master chose not to live at Warkworth. He sold off the entire estate by public auction on 18 June 1805. The advertisement read: AUCTION SALE. Valuable freehold Manor Estate, tythe free by Messrs. Winstanley & Son, at Garraway's this day 18th June, at 12 o'clock, in one lot. Warkworth Castle, with the Manor and Estate, situate in the County of Northampton on the verge of the northern part of Oxfordshire, 2 miles from Banbury, 22 miles from Oxford, 27 miles from Coventry, 20 miles from Northampton, 70 miles from London, consisting of a mansion house and offices, with the park and lands, plantations, fishponds, and matter in hand. Four capital farms, well-timbered, occupied by the most respectable tenants from year to year, capable of great improvement, and about 13 dwelling houses in the village of Overthorpe adjoining the Park. The Estate, which is in a ring fence, contains 1073 acres of land, a very small proportion of which is arable, the rest meadows and pasture, tythe free, bounded on one side by the River Cherwell, over which there is right of fishery. Possession may be had of the mansion and 100 acres of land immediately and of the remainder at Lady-day 1806.'

The 'mansion and estate' were bought by Mr Thomas Bradford for £53,000, a very considerable sum in 1805, when a maid-of-all-work could earn about £5 a year. He cared nothing for the expense, however, and was doubtless unconcerned by any credit he had to arrange in order to meet it, because he had no intention of making the 'great improvement' suggested by the estate agent. He set about straight away to selling off the interior fittings of the castle, and after Lord Newburgh had collected the last rents on the March quarter-day in 1806, he parcelled the estate into smaller lots for a quick-return re-sale. Warkworth Castle was intentionally demolished in 1806.

The lots nearest the village were purchased by local yeomen. Mr Taylor bought much of the land and erected the date stone from above the castle entrance in his garden. G. Baker observed it there when he visited the village in 1822 while writing *History and Antiquities of the County of Northamptonshire*, and he describes it as bearing the date 1595 and the Chetwode coat of arms. Mr Osbourne bought one of the 'capital farms'; an inventory of land sale survives in the collection of the residents of Dove House in Warkworth. Dated 'the sixth day of January in the forty-ninth year of the reign of our Sovereign Lord George the Third [1809]', it describes a land sale from Thomas Bradford, Gent, of Sussex to John Osbourne, Yeoman, of Warkworth, and a sketch map in the left-hand margin of one page shows exactly where the boundaries joined the lands of Mr Drury and the aforementioned Mr Taylor. It concerns 'all that plot of land situate and being in the Parish of Warkworth aforesaid containing by Statute Measure twelve acres or thereabouts little more or less bounded on the north by lands now belonging to William Barret on the south by lands belonging to William Drury and on the east by the road leading from Warkworth aforesaid to Middleton Cheney and on the west by lands now belonging to Richard Mumford ... on which plot of land a Castle called Warkworth Castle which hath been ... demolished lately stood ...'

Osbourne (who signs himself 'Orsborne' perhaps revealing a local accent) bought the plot 'at the price or sum of £600 of Lawful English money to the said Thomas Bradford in hand well and truly paid'. The lack of a local magnate seemed to be signalling the rise of the local yeomen; Thomas Mawle, who had been renting from Lord Newburgh for years, also purchased his farm in 1806, and Warkworth Farm contains carved oak panelling which, family tradition says, came from the castle. However, the inhabitants of the village did not have many years to enjoy their good fortune, because two years later in 1811, the disaster feared by all farmers destroyed homes and livelihoods in a terrifying conflagration. The tragedy was reported in Jackson's *Oxford Journal*: 'On Friday the 20th inst. a most destructive Fire broke out at the Dwelling house of Mr Robert Taylor of Warkworth near Banbury which burnt down the same also the Dwelling house of Mr Osbourne with all extensive barns and outbuildings of Messrs Osbourne Maull and Drury. The Fire was carried by the Violence of the Wind to a Dwelling house some yards Distance which was consumed. The Cries of a valuable Mare in foal, Pigs etc. which were Burnt were truly Distressful. The Loss in corn, hay and goods was very great and Insured for a small Amount. Only one house could be Saved and that had taken fire. Four Engines attended but could Save a very small part of household

Goods, Stock etc. Notwithstanding the Exertions of Banbury Inhabitants and the Engines from thence, the Wind was so high that in less than Two Hours the Village was nearly Burnt down. We are sorry to say Mr Osbourne was Severely Burnt.'

Sure enough, only one house in Warkworth can be dated to earlier than the nineteenth century. John Osbourne only lived a few more years, dying in 1814; we cannot tell whether the injuries he sustained fighting the fire effectively shortened his life or not. The Taylors, residents in the village since the sixteenth century, died out too within a few years; their family tomb stands in the churchyard opposite the transept door, almost buried under thick ivy. As the whole nation celebrated the victory over Napoleon in 1815, the residents of Warkworth were still rebuilding their homes and their lives. The house that was saved belonged to the Mawle family, and they still live there today.

When F. Whellan surveyed Warkworth in 1874 for his book *History, Topography and Directory of Northamptonshire*, he found only three farmhouses and one cottage. However, as with farming the land often yields best after some years lying fallow, so it seems to have been with Warkworth. The village is now home to many more people due to new building in the early part of the twentieth century and the more recent barn conversions. Through the several businesses based there, it provides many local people with employment, and although you can't come and look around the castle, St Mary's church, containing monuments dating back to the fourteenth century, is well worth a visit.

Shona Rutherford-Edge

CHAPTER 9
Images of Banbury

On 19 April 1912 the Banbury Scout troop collected over £12 for the Titanic Disaster Fund. This photograph, taken in South Bar, includes Norman Blinkhorn (left), Bernard Blinkhorn (right), and Don Braggins, Norman's brother-in-law. In the background the statue of the Banbury Cross had been draped in black cloth as a mark of respect for those who had perished. (Supplied and researched by Martin Blinkhorn)

Banbury High Street during the celebrations for Queen Victoria's Diamond Jubilee in 1897. (Supplied by Martin Blinkhorn)

Harlequin and Goggin the bakers at Nos 47 and 48 High Street, Banbury.(Supplied by Christine Wells)

The Wagon and Horses pub in Butchers Row. This still trades as a pub, but is now known as The Banbury Cross. (Supplied by Martin Blinkhorn)

St Mary's church on North Bar, before the First World War. (Supplied by Martin Blinkhorn)

The Post Office Float in the Diamond Jubilee celebrations of 1897, in Dashwood Road. (Supplied by Martin Blinkhorn)

This picture shows the Original Cake Shop in parsons Street. It is likely that it was taken during the celebrations of Queen Victoria's Diamond Jubilee in 1897.

Part of the right-hand side of Market Place, looking down towards the Town Hall building. It shows the Fox Inn, Hills & Rowney (the first art shop in Banbury), and Neal's shoe store. Above them is the site of the old Gaol. (Supplied by Martin Blinkhorn)

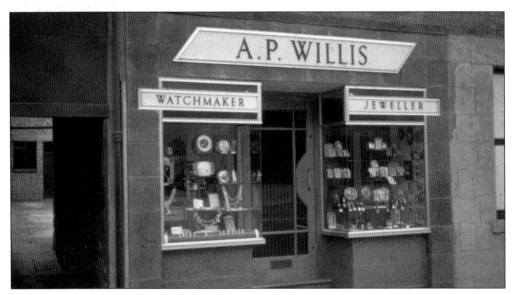

A.P. Willis, No. 14 Bridge Street in the 1970s. (Supplied by Christine Wells)

Banbury High Street, 1930. The buildings on the left-hand corner of the picture still exist, though the tailor and outfitter, and the ironmonger are now trading as a travel agents and key-cutting store. (Supplied by Martin Blinkhorn)

South Bar, looking down to Banbury Cross, in the early twentieth century. In the right-hand corner of the picture we can see two ladies looking through the window of Beales' photographic shop. (Supplied by Martin Blinkhorn)

*Wincott's Café, South Bar, 1938.
During the Second World War
American soldiers were billeted here.
(Supplied by Martin Blinkhorn)*

During the construction of Castle Quay Shopping Centre, which opened in summer 2000.

Marlborough Road, 1900s. St Mary's church can be seen in the middle distance. (Supplied by Christine Wells)

The Crown public house in Warwick Road, during the 1960s. This was the site of the old people's bungalows. (Supplied by Christine Wells)

Hoods and alleyway to Factory Street, c. 1973. Hoods is an ironmonger's which sells household goods and garden implements and is still trading today. (Supplied by Christine Wells)

Norland octagonal house at Balscote. The house was designed in 1958. (Supplied by Christine Wells)

A view from the north side of the market place, from the roof of the Palace Cinema. (Supplied by Christine Wells)

Marlborough Road Methodist church before the demolition of the schoolroom section. (Supplied by Christine Wells)

Ottakar's LOCAL HISTORY *Series*

Banbury

This photograph appeared in the 'Memory Lane' section of the local newspaper. The annual hospital carnival was eagerly looked forward to. Everyone made a great effort to make this one of the highlights on the town's calendar. Jack Gilkes is dressed as Old Mother Riley, and Grace Gilkes is seated in the pram with her cousin Annie Newton. The fancy dress procession used to go all over Grimsbury and then finish up in the hospital. Much thought went into this very enjoyable occasion. (Supplied and researched by Grace Plester)